GOVERNMENT PROCEDURES AND OPERATIONS

VIRTUAL CURRENCIES

REGULATORY AND TAX COMPLIANCE ISSUES

GOVERNMENT PROCEDURES AND OPERATIONS

Additional books in this series can be found on Nova's website under the Series tab.

Additional e-books in this series can be found on Nova's website under the e-book tab.

GOVERNMENT PROCEDURES AND OPERATIONS

VIRTUAL CURRENCIES

REGULATORY AND TAX COMPLIANCE ISSUES

KEVIN LYNDELL
EDITOR

nova publishers
New York

For permission to use material from this book please contact us:
Telephone 631-231-7269; Fax 631-231-8175
Web Site: http://www.novapublishers.com

Library of Congress Cataloging-in-Publication Data

ISBN: 978-1-63463-129-7

Published by Nova Science Publishers, Inc. † New York

CONTENTS

PREFACE

This book discusses federal financial regulatory and law enforcement agency responsibilities related to the use of virtual currencies and associated challenges; actions and collaborative efforts the agencies have undertaken regarding virtual currencies; describes the tax reporting requirements for virtual economies and currencies; identifies the potential tax compliance risks of virtual economies and currencies; and assesses how IRS has addressed the tax compliance risks of virtual economies and currencies.

Chapter 1 - Virtual currencies—digital representations of value that are not government-issued—have grown in popularity in recent years. Some virtual currencies can be used to buy real goods and services and exchanged for dollars or other currencies. One example of these is bitcoin, which was developed in 2009. Bitcoin and similar virtual currency systems operate over the Internet and use computer protocols and encryption to conduct and verify transactions. While these virtual currency systems offer some benefits, they also pose risks. For example, they have been associated with illicit activity and security breaches, raising possible regulatory, law enforcement, and consumer protection issues. GAO was asked to examine federal policy and interagency collaboration issues concerning virtual currencies.

This report discusses (1) federal financial regulatory and law enforcement agency responsibilities related to the use of virtual currencies and associated challenges and (2) actions and collaborative efforts the agencies have undertaken regarding virtual currencies. To address these objectives, GAO reviewed federal laws and regulations, academic and industry research, and agency documents; and interviewed federal agency officials, researchers, and industry groups.

Chapter 2 - Recent years have seen the development of virtual economies, such as those within online role-playing games, through which individual participants can own and exchange virtual goods and services. Within some virtual economies, virtual currencies have been created as a medium of exchange for goods and services. Virtual property and currency can be exchanged for real goods, services, and currency, and virtual currencies have been developed outside of virtual economies as alternatives to government-issued currencies, such as dollars. These innovations raise questions about related tax requirements and potential challenges for IRS compliance efforts.

This report (1) describes the tax reporting requirements for virtual economies and currencies, (2) identifies the potential tax compliance risks of virtual economies and currencies, and (3) assesses how IRS has addressed the tax compliance risks of virtual economies and currencies.

To accomplish these objectives, GAO reviewed tax laws, IRS guidance and program documents, federal program internal control guidance, and interviewed IRS officials and knowledgeable experts on the topics.

Chapter 3 - The Financial Crimes Enforcement Network ("FinCEN") is issuing this interpretive guidance to clarify the applicability of the regulations implementing the Bank Secrecy Act ("BSA") to persons creating, obtaining, distributing, exchanging, accepting, or transmitting virtual currencies. Such persons are referred to in this guidance as "users," "administrators," and "exchangers,". A user of virtual currency is ***not*** an MSB under FinCEN's regulations and therefore is not subject to MSB registration, reporting, and recordkeeping regulations. However, an administrator or exchanger ***is*** an MSB under FinCEN's regulations, specifically, a money transmitter, unless a limitation to or exemption from the definition applies to the person. An administrator or exchanger is not a provider or seller of prepaid access, or a dealer in foreign exchange, under FinCEN's regulations.

Chapter 4 - This is an edited, reformatted and augmented version of regulatory document, FIN-2014-R001, issued by the U.S. Department of the Treasury, Financial Crimes Enforcement Network, January 30, 2014.

Chapter 5 - This is an edited, reformatted and augmented version of regulatory document, FIN-2014-R002, issued by the U.S. Department of the Treasury, Financial Crimes Enforcement Network, January 30, 2014.

Chapter 6 - This is an edited, reformatted and augmented version of regulatory document, FIN-2014-R007, issued by the U.S. Department of the Treasury, Financial Crimes Enforcement Network, April 29, 2014.

Chapter 7 - Bitcoin first appeared in January 2009, the creation of a computer programmer using the pseudonym Satoshi Nakamoto. His invention is an open source (its controlling computer code is open to public view), peer to peer (transactions do not require a third-party intermediary such as PayPal or Visa), digital currency (being electronic with no physical manifestation). The Bitcoin system is private, but with no traditional financial institutions involved in transactions. Unlike earlier digital currencies that had some central controlling person or entity, the Bitcoin network is *completely decentralized*, with all parts of transactions performed by the users of the system.

With a Bitcoin transaction there is no third party intermediary. The buyer and seller interact directly (peer to peer) but their identities are encrypted and no personal information is transferred from one to the other. However, unlike a fully anonymous transaction, there is a transaction record. A full transaction record of every Bitcoin and every Bitcoin user's encrypted identity is maintained on the public ledger. For this reason Bitcoin transactions are thought to be pseudonymous, not anonymous. Although the scale of Bitcoin use has increased substantially, it still remains small in comparison to traditional electronic payments systems such as credit cards and the use of dollars as a circulating currency.

Congress is interested in Bitcoin because of concerns about its use in illegal money transfers, concerns about its effect on the ability of the Federal Reserve to meet its objectives (of stable prices, maximum employment, and financial stability), and concerns about the protection of consumers and investors who might use it.

Bitcoin offers users the advantages of lower transaction costs, increased privacy, and long term protection of loss of purchasing power from inflation. However, there are also a number of disadvantages that could hinder wider use. These include sizable volatility of the price of Bitcoins, uncertain security from theft and fraud, and a long term deflationary bias that encourages the hoarding of Bitcoins.

Bitcoin also raises a number of legal and regulatory concerns including its potential for facilitating money laundering, its treatment under federal securities law, and its status in the regulation of foreign exchange trading.

In: Virtual Currencies
Editor: Kevin Lyndell
ISBN: 978-1-63463-129-7

Chapter 1

VIRTUAL CURRENCIES: EMERGING REGULATORY, LAW ENFORCEMENT, AND CONSUMER PROTECTION CHALLENGES*

United States Government Accountability Office

WHY GAO DID THIS STUDY

Virtual currencies—digital representations of value that are not government-issued—have grown in popularity in recent years. Some virtual currencies can be used to buy real goods and services and exchanged for dollars or other currencies. One example of these is bitcoin, which was developed in 2009. Bitcoin and similar virtual currency systems operate over the Internet and use computer protocols and encryption to conduct and verify transactions. While these virtual currency systems offer some benefits, they also pose risks. For example, they have been associated with illicit activity and security breaches, raising possible regulatory, law enforcement, and consumer protection issues. GAO was asked to examine federal policy and interagency collaboration issues concerning virtual currencies.

This report discusses (1) federal financial regulatory and law enforcement agency responsibilities related to the use of virtual currencies and associated challenges and (2) actions and collaborative efforts the agencies have

---

* This is an edited, reformatted and augmented version of the United States Government Accountability Office publication, GAO-14-496, dated May 2014.

undertaken regarding virtual currencies. To address these objectives, GAO reviewed federal laws and regulations, academic and industry research, and agency documents; and interviewed federal agency officials, researchers, and industry groups.

WHAT GAO RECOMMENDS

GAO recommends that CFPB take steps to identify and participate in pertinent interagency working groups addressing virtual currencies, in coordination with other participating agencies. CFPB concurred with this recommendation.

WHAT GAO FOUND

Virtual currencies are financial innovations that pose emerging challenges to federal financial regulatory and law enforcement agencies in carrying out their responsibilities, as the following examples illustrate:

- Virtual currency systems may provide greater anonymity than traditional payment systems and sometimes lack a central intermediary to maintain transaction information. As a result, financial regulators and law enforcement agencies may find it difficult to detect money laundering and other crimes involving virtual currencies.
- Many virtual currency systems can be accessed globally to make payments and transfer funds across borders. Consequently, law enforcement agencies investigating and prosecuting crimes that involve virtual currencies may have to rely upon cooperation from international partners who may operate under different regulatory and legal regimes.
- The emergence of virtual currencies has raised a number of consumer and investor protection issues. These include the reported loss of consumer funds maintained by bitcoin exchanges, volatility in bitcoin prices, and the development of virtual-currency-based investment products. For example, in February 2014, a Tokyo-based bitcoin

exchange called Mt. Gox filed for bankruptcy after reporting that it had lost more than $460 million.

Federal financial regulatory and law enforcement agencies have taken a number of actions regarding virtual currencies. In March 2013, the Department of the Treasury's Financial Crimes Enforcement Network (FinCEN) issued guidance that clarified which participants in virtual currency systems are subject to anti-money-laundering requirements and required virtual currency exchanges to register with FinCEN. Additionally, financial regulators have taken some actions regarding anti-money-laundering compliance and investor protection. For example, in July 2013, the Securities and Exchange Commission (SEC) charged an individual and his company with defrauding investors through a bitcoin-based investment scheme. Further, law enforcement agencies have taken actions against parties alleged to have used virtual currencies to facilitate money laundering or other crimes. For example, in October 2013, multiple agencies worked together to shut down Silk Road, an online marketplace where users paid for illegal goods and services with bitcoins.

Federal agencies also have begun to collaborate on virtual currency issues through informal discussions and interagency working groups primarily concerned with money laundering and other law enforcement matters. However, these working groups have not focused on emerging consumer protection issues, and the Consumer Financial Protection Bureau (CFPB)—whose responsibilities include providing consumers with information to make responsible decisions about financial transactions—has generally not participated in these groups. Therefore, interagency efforts related to virtual currencies may not be consistent with key practices that can benefit interagency collaboration, such as including all relevant participants to ensure they contribute to the outcomes of the effort. As a result, future interagency efforts may not be in a position to address consumer risks associated with virtual currencies in the most timely and effective manner.

ABBREVIATIONS

BSA	Bank Secrecy Act
BSAAG	Bank Secrecy Act Advisory Group
CFPB	Consumer Financial Protection Bureau
CFTC	Commodity Futures Trading Commission

DATA	Digital Asset Transfer Authority
DEA	Drug Enforcement Administration
DHS	Department of Homeland Security
DOJ	Department of Justice
ECTF	Electronic Crimes Task Forces
EFTA	Electronic Fund Transfer Act
FATF	Financial Action Task Force
FBI	Federal Bureau of Investigation
FDIC	Federal Deposit Insurance Corporation
FFIEC	Federal Financial Institutions Examination Council
FinCEN	Financial Crimes Enforcement Network
HSI	Homeland Security Investigations
ICE	U.S. Immigration and Customs Enforcement
IOC-2	International Organized Crime Intelligence and Operations Center
IRS	Internal Revenue Service
IRS	Internal Revenue Service
NCUA	National Credit Union Administration
OCC	Office of the Comptroller of the Currency
SEC	Securities and Exchange Commission
TOR	The Onion Router
USAID	United States Agency for International Development
VCET	Virtual Currency Emerging Threats Working Group

***

May 29, 2014

The Honorable Thomas R. Carper
Chairman

The Honorable Tom A. Coburn
Ranking Member
Committee on Homeland Security and Governmental Affairs
United States Senate

While not widely used or accepted, virtual currencies, such as bitcoin, have grown in popularity in recent years and have emerged for some as potential alternatives to traditional currencies issued by governments. Virtual currencies operate over the Internet and, in some cases, may be used to buy real goods and services and exchanged for traditional currencies. They offer potential benefits over traditional currencies, including lower transaction costs and faster funds transfers. Because some virtual currency transactions provide greater anonymity than transactions using traditional payment systems, law enforcement and financial regulators have raised concerns about the use of virtual currencies for illegal activities. Additionally, recent cases involving the loss of funds from virtual currency exchanges have highlighted potential consumer protection issues.

You asked us to examine potential policy issues related to virtual currencies and the status of federal agency collaboration in this area. This report focuses on the federal financial regulatory agencies and selected federal law enforcement agencies that have a role in protecting the U.S. financial system and investigating financial crimes.[1] Specifically, this report addresses (1) agency responsibilities related to the use of virtual currencies and the emerging challenges these currencies pose to the agencies; and (2) actions the agencies have taken in response to the emergence of virtual currencies, including interagency collaborative efforts. We selected the law enforcement agencies included in our review based on their involvement in investigating virtual-currency-related crimes and participation in interagency collaborative efforts and congressional hearings on virtual currency issues.

To describe agency responsibilities related to the use of virtual currencies and the emerging challenges these currencies pose, we reviewed the following agency information: testimony and written statements from relevant congressional hearings, written responses to congressional questions, unclassified intelligence assessments, financial reports, training presentations, and descriptions of missions and responsibilities from agencies' websites.[2] We also reviewed prior GAO reports, Congressional Research Service reports, and relevant laws and regulations, including the Bank Secrecy Act (BSA) and related anti-money laundering provisions such as Title III of the USA PATRIOT Act, to gain an understanding of agencies' responsibilities in administering and enforcing anti-money-laundering laws and regulations, as well as in investigating and prosecuting financial and other crimes.[3] In addition, we reviewed academic articles and papers from industry stakeholders. Further, we interviewed officials from the following federal financial regulatory and law enforcement agencies:

- The Board of Governors of the Federal Reserve System (Federal Reserve);
- The Bureau of Consumer Financial Protection (also known as the Consumer Financial Protection Bureau or CFPB);
- The Commodity Futures Trading Commission (CFTC);
- The Department of Homeland Security (DHS), including U.S. Immigration and Customs Enforcement–Homeland Security Investigations (ICE-HSI) and the U.S. Secret Service (Secret Service);
- The Department of Justice (DOJ), including the Criminal Division and two of its components—the Asset Forfeiture and Money Laundering Section and Computer Crime and Intellectual Property Section—and the Federal Bureau of Investigation (FBI);
- The Department of the Treasury (Treasury), including the Financial Crimes Enforcement Network (FinCEN) and the Office of the Comptroller of the Currency (OCC);
- The Federal Deposit Insurance Corporation (FDIC);
- The National Credit Union Administration (NCUA); and
- The Securities and Exchange Commission (SEC).

Additionally, we interviewed an academic whose research focused on virtual currencies and industry stakeholders, including the Bitcoin Foundation, the Digital Asset Transfer Authority (DATA), and the National Money Transmitters Association, which represent the interests of a large number of virtual currency and money transmission businesses.

To examine the actions and collaborative efforts federal agencies have undertaken in response to the emergence of virtual currencies, we reviewed agency information, including FinCEN's regulatory guidance and administrative rulings on the applicability of BSA to virtual currency participants, testimony and written statements from the previously mentioned congressional hearings, written responses to congressional questions, intelligence assessments, a CFPB query of its Consumer Complaint Database, and press releases.[4] We also interviewed officials from the agencies listed previously to obtain further information on the actions they have taken to address the emergence of virtual currencies and their efforts to collaborate with other federal agencies on this issue. Additionally, we interviewed the academic and industry stakeholders noted previously, as well as the Digital Economy Task Force, to determine the extent to which private sector groups were involved in interagency collaborative efforts.[5] We reviewed GAO's key practices on collaboration and assessed whether interagency collaborative efforts related to virtual currencies were consistent with practices concerning the inclusion of relevant participants.[6]

We conducted this performance audit from November 2013 to May 2014 in accordance with generally accepted government auditing standards. Those standards require that we plan and perform the audit to obtain sufficient, appropriate evidence to provide a reasonable basis for our findings and conclusions based on our audit objectives. We believe that the evidence obtained provides a reasonable basis for our findings and conclusions based on our audit objectives.

BACKGROUND

Virtual currencies are financial innovations that have grown in number and popularity in recent years. While there is no statutory definition for virtual currency, the term refers to a digital representation of value that is not government-issued legal tender. Unlike U.S. dollars and other government-issued currencies, virtual currencies do not necessarily have a physical coin or bill associated with their circulation. While virtual currencies can function as a unit of account, store of value, and medium of exchange, they are not widely used or accepted. Some virtual currencies can only be used within virtual economies (for example, within online role-playing games) and may not be readily exchanged for government-issued currencies such as U.S. dollars, euro, or yen. Other virtual currencies may be used to purchase goods and services in the real economy and can be converted into government-issued currencies through virtual currency exchanges. In previous work, we described the latter type of virtual currencies as "open flow."[7] Open-flow virtual currencies have received considerable attention from federal financial regulatory and law enforcement agencies, in part because these currencies interact with the real economy and because depository institutions (for example, banks and credit unions) may have business relationships with companies that exchange virtual currencies for government-issued currencies. Throughout the remainder of this report, we use the term virtual currencies to mean open-flow virtual currencies, unless otherwise stated.[8]

Virtual currency systems, which include protocols for conducting transactions in addition to digital representations of value, can either be centralized or decentralized. Centralized virtual currency systems have a single administering authority that issues the currency and has the authority to withdraw the currency from circulation. In addition, the administrating authority issues rules for use of the currency and maintains a central payment ledger. In contrast, decentralized virtual currency systems have no central administering authority. Validation and certification of transactions are performed by users of the system and therefore do not require a third party to perform intermediation activities.

A prominent example of a decentralized virtual currency system is bitcoin. Bitcoin was developed in 2009 by an unidentified programmer or programmers using the name Satoshi Nakamoto. According to industry stakeholders, bitcoin is the most widely circulated decentralized virtual currency. The bitcoin computer protocol permits the storage of unique digital representations of value (bitcoins) and facilitates the assignment of bitcoins from one user to another through a peer-to-peer, Internet-based network.[9] Each bitcoin is divisible to eight decimal places, enabling their use in any kind of transaction regardless of the value. Users' bitcoin balances are associated with bitcoin addresses (long strings of numbers and letters) that use principles of cryptography to help safeguard against inappropriate tampering with bitcoin transactions and balances.[10] When users transfer bitcoins, the recipient provides their bitcoin address to the sender, and the sender authorizes the transaction with their private key (essentially a secret code that proves the sender's control over their bitcoin address). Bitcoin transactions are irrevocable and do not require the sender or receiver to disclose their identities to each other or a third party. However, each transaction is registered in a public ledger called the "blockchain," which maintains the associated bitcoin addresses and transaction dates, times, and amounts. Users can define how much additional information they require of each other to conduct a transaction.

Because peer-to-peer bitcoin transactions do not require the disclosure of information about a user's identity, they give the participants some degree of anonymity. In addition, computer network communication can be encrypted and anonymized by software to further hide the identity of the parties in transactions.[11] However, the transactions are not completely anonymous because the time and amount of each transaction and the associated bitcoin addresses are permanently recorded in the blockchain. As a result, peer-to-peer bitcoin transactions are sometimes described as "pseudonymous." The anonymity of bitcoin is also limited by data analysis techniques that can potentially link bitcoin addresses to personal identities. For example, information about a customer's identity may be recorded when an individual exchanges dollars for bitcoins, and this information may be combined with data from the blockchain to determine the identities of participants in bitcoin transactions. In addition, researchers have developed methods to determine identities of parties involved in some bitcoin transactions by analyzing clusters of transactions between specific addresses.[12]

Bitcoins are created and entered into circulation through a process called mining. Bitcoin miners download free software that they use to solve complex math problems. Solving these problems verifies the validity of bitcoin transactions by grouping several transactions into a block and mathematically proving that the transactions occurred and did not involve double spending of a bitcoin. On average, this process takes about 10 minutes. When a miner or group of miners (mining pools) solves a problem, the bitcoin network accepts the block of transactions as valid and creates new bitcoins and awards them to the successful miner or mining pool.[13] (For a diagram on how bitcoins enter into circulation through mining, how transactions are conducted, and how miners verify transactions, see app. I.) Over time, the computer processing power needed to mine new bitcoins has increased to the point where mining requires specialized computer hardware and has become increasingly consolidated into large mining pools.

In addition to mining new bitcoins, users can also acquire bitcoins already in circulation by accepting bitcoins as gifts or payments for goods or services, purchasing them at bitcoin kiosks (sometimes referred to as bitcoin automated teller machines), or purchasing them on third-party exchanges. These exchanges allow users to exchange traditional currencies such as U.S. dollars for bitcoins, and exchange bitcoins back to traditional currencies. Individuals may store their bitcoins in a "virtual wallet" (a program that saves bitcoin addresses) on their computer or other data storage device, or use an online wallet service provided by an exchange or third-party virtual wallet provider. To spend their bitcoins, individuals can buy goods or services from other bitcoin users. They may also make purchases from online businesses that either accept bitcoins directly or use third-party payment processors that take payments in bitcoins from buyers and provide businesses the payments in the form of a traditional currency or a combination of bitcoins and traditional currency. Figure 1 shows various ways that individuals can obtain and spend bitcoins.

Due to limitations in available data, the size of the bitcoin market is unclear.[14] Nonetheless, some data exist that may provide some context for the size of this market:

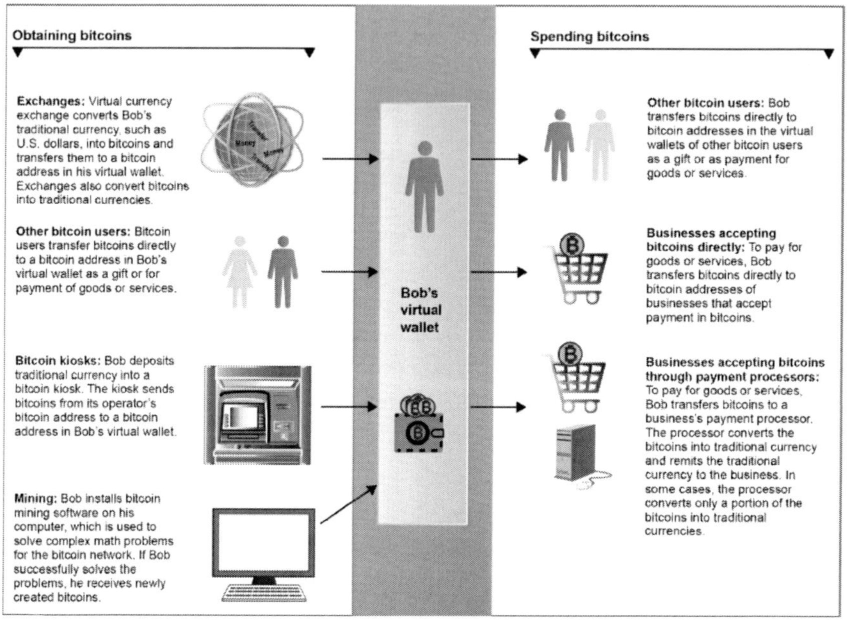

Source: GAO.

Figure 1. Ways to Obtain and Spend Bitcoins.

- According to statistics from the bitcoin blockchain, as of March 31, 2014, approximately 12.6 million bitcoins were in circulation.[15]
- At exchange rates as of March 31, 2014 (about $458 per bitcoin), the total value of the approximately 12.6 million bitcoins in circulation was about $5.6 billion.[16] For perspective, the total amount of U.S. currency held by the public and in transaction deposits (mainly checking accounts) at depository institutions was about $2.7 trillion as of March 2014.[17]
- Bitcoin exchange rates against the U.S. dollar have changed dramatically over time (see figure 2). According to one bitcoin price index, the price was about $13 per bitcoin in the beginning of January 2013 and rose to more than $1,100 by the beginning of December 2013. Prices subsequently fell to about $522 in mid-December 2013 and have fluctuated between roughly $450 and $950 since then.[18]
- From April 2013 through March 2014, the number of bitcoin transactions per day ranged from about 29,000 to 102,000.[19] In

comparison, the Federal Reserve Banks processed an average of 44 million commercial Automated Clearing House (a traditional payment processor) transactions per day in 2013.[20]

While bitcoin is the most widely used virtual currency, numerous others have been created. For example, dozens of decentralized virtual currencies are based on the bitcoin protocol such as Litecoin, Auroracoin, Peercoin, and Dogecoin. Similar to the bitcoin market, the size of the market for these virtual currencies is unclear. However, as of March 31, 2014, the total reported value of each of these currencies was less than $400 million (ranging from about $33 million for Dogecoin to about $346 million for Litecoin).[21] Other virtual currencies that have been created are not based on the bitcoin protocol. One of the more prominent examples is XRP, which is used within a decentralized payment system called Ripple. Ripple allows users to make peer-to-peer transfers in any currency. A key function of XRP is to facilitate the conversion from one currency to another. For example, if a direct conversion between Mexican pesos and Thai baht is not available, the pesos can be exchanged for XRP, and then the XRP for baht. As of March 31, 2014, the total value of XRP was $878 million.[22]

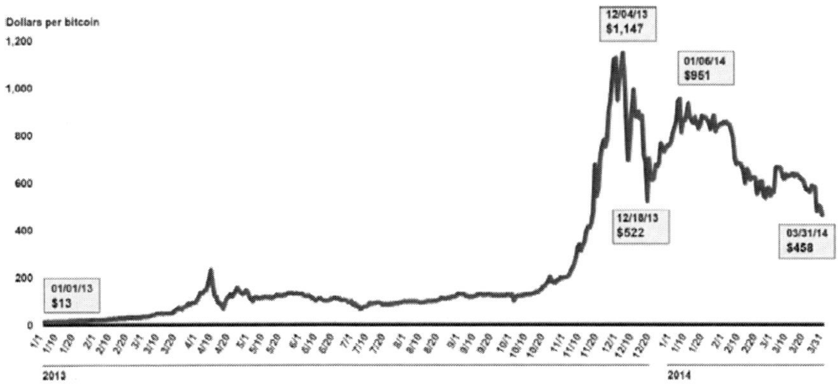

Source: GAO analysis of data from http://www.coindesk.com/price (accessed on Apr. 1, 2014).

Note: The index is a composite price calculated as the simple average of bitcoin prices across leading global exchanges that meet certain criteria. The values are expressed in current U.S. dollars.

Figure 2. Bitcoin Price Index in U.S. Dollars, January 1, 2013 through March 31, 2014.

Virtual currencies have drawn attention from federal agencies with responsibilities for protecting the U.S. financial system and its participants and investigating financial crimes. These include, but are not limited to, CFPB, CFTC, DHS, DOJ, SEC, Treasury, and the prudential banking regulators. The prudential banking regulators are the FDIC, Federal Reserve, NCUA, and OCC. Within Treasury, FinCEN has a particular interest in the emergence of virtual currencies because of concerns about the use of these currencies for money laundering and FinCEN's role in combating such activity.[23] Additionally, because virtual currencies (like government-issued currencies) can play a role in a range of financial and other crimes, including cross-border criminal activity, key components of DOJ and DHS have an interest in how virtual currencies are used. Relevant DOJ components include the Criminal Division (which oversees the Computer Crime and Intellectual Property Section and the Asset Forfeiture and Money Laundering Section), the FBI, and the Offices of the U.S. Attorneys (U.S. Attorneys). Relevant DHS components include the Secret Service and ICE-HSI.

FEDERAL AGENCIES FACE EMERGING CHALLENGES IN CARRYING OUT RESPONSIBILITIES RELATED TO THE USE OF VIRTUAL CURRENCIES

While federal agencies' responsibilities with respect to virtual currency are still being clarified, some virtual currency activities and products have implications for the responsibilities of federal financial regulatory and law enforcement agencies. Virtual currencies have presented these agencies with emerging challenges as they carry out their different responsibilities. These challenges stem partly from certain characteristics of virtual currency systems, such as the higher degree of anonymity they provide compared with traditional payment systems and the ease with which they can be accessed globally to make payments and transfer funds across borders.

Some Virtual Currency Activities and Products May Have Implications for Federal Agencies' Responsibilities

Although virtual currencies are not government-issued and do not currently pass through U.S. banks, some activities and products that involve virtual currencies have implications for the responsibilities of federal financial regulatory and law enforcement agencies. These activities and products encompass both legitimate and illegitimate uses of virtual currencies. Examples of legitimate uses include buying virtual currencies and registered virtual-currency-denominated investment products. Examples of illegitimate uses include money laundering and purchasing illegal goods and services using virtual currencies.

FinCEN

FinCEN administers BSA and its implementing regulations.[24] The goal of BSA is to prevent financial institutions from being used as intermediaries for the transfer or deposit of money derived from criminal activity and to provide a paper trail to assist law enforcement agencies in their money laundering investigations. To the extent that entities engaged in money transmission conduct virtual currency transactions with U.S. customers or become customers of a U.S. financial institution, FinCEN has responsibilities for helping ensure that these entities comply with BSA and anti-money-laundering regulations.[25]

FinCEN regulations set forth requirements for money services businesses, which include financial institutions and other entities engaged in money transmission.[26] FinCEN guidance states that the agency's regulations regarding money services businesses apply to virtual currency exchangers and administrators.[27] FinCEN applies its regulations to "convertible virtual currency," which either has an equivalent value in real currency or acts as a substitute for real currency. FinCEN regulations require money services businesses to assess their exposure to money laundering and terrorist financing and establish risk mitigation plans in the form of anti-money-laundering programs.[28] Additionally, money services businesses are required to maintain transaction records. For example, for money transfers that are $3,000 or more, money services businesses must obtain information on the transmitter, the recipient, and the transaction itself, and pass on such information to other intermediary financial institutions in any subsequent fund transmissions. Money services businesses are also required to monitor transactions and file reports on large currency transactions and suspicious activities. In addition, certain financial institutions must establish a written customer identification program that includes procedures for obtaining minimum identification information from customers who open an account, such as date of birth, a government identification number, and physical address.[29] Further, financial institutions must file currency transaction reports on customer cash transactions exceeding $10,000 that include information about the account owner's identity and occupation.[30]

FinCEN also supports the investigative and prosecutive efforts of multiple federal and state law enforcement agencies through its administration of the financial transaction reporting and recordkeeping requirements mandated or authorized under BSA. In addition, FinCEN has the authority to take enforcement actions, such as assessing civil money penalties, against financial institutions, including money services businesses, that violate BSA requirements.

Prudential Banking Regulators

The prudential banking regulators—FDIC, Federal Reserve, NCUA, and OCC—provide oversight of depository institutions' compliance with BSA and anti-money-laundering requirements. Therefore, these regulators are responsible for providing guidance and oversight to help ensure that depository institutions that have opened accounts for virtual currency exchanges or other money services businesses have adequate anti-money-laundering controls for those accounts.[31] In April 2005, FinCEN and the prudential banking regulators issued joint guidance to banking organizations (depository institutions and bank holding companies) to clarify BSA requirements with respect to money services businesses and to set forth the minimum steps that banking organizations should take when providing banking services to these businesses.[32] As part of safety and soundness or targeted BSA compliance examinations of depository institutions, the prudential banking regulators assess compliance with BSA and related anti-money-laundering requirements using procedures that are consistent with their overall risk-focused examination approach.[33] In examining depository institutions for BSA compliance, the regulators review whether depository institutions (1) have developed anti-money-laundering programs and procedures to detect and report unusual or suspicious activities possibly related to money laundering; and (2) comply with the technical recordkeeping and reporting requirements of BSA.[34] While most cases of BSA noncompliance are corrected within the examination framework, regulators can take a range of supervisory actions, including formal enforcement actions, against the entities they supervise for violations of BSA and anti-money-laundering requirements. These formal enforcement actions can include imposing civil money penalties and initiating cease-and-desist proceedings.[35]

Consumer Financial Protection Bureau

CFPB is an independent entity within the Federal Reserve that has broad consumer protection responsibilities over an array of consumer financial products and services, including taking deposits and transferring money. CFPB is responsible for enforcing federal consumer protection laws, and it is the primary consumer protection supervisor over many of the institutions that offer consumer financial products and services. CFPB also has authority to issue and revise regulations that implement federal consumer financial protection laws, including the Electronic Fund Transfer Act[36] and title X of the Dodd-Frank Wall Street Reform and Consumer Protection Act (Dodd-Frank Act).[37] CFPB officials stated that they are reviewing how these responsibilities are implicated by consumer use (or potential consumer use) of virtual currencies.

Other relevant CFPB responsibilities concerning virtual currencies include accepting and handling consumer complaints, promoting financial education, researching consumer behavior, and monitoring financial markets for new risks to consumers. For example, under authorities provided by the Dodd-Frank Act, CFPB maintains a Consumer Complaint Database and helps monitor and assess risks to consumers in the offering or provision of consumer financial products or services.[38] CFPB also issues consumer advisories to promote clarity, transparency, and fairness in consumer financial markets.

Securities and Exchange Commission

SEC regulates the securities markets—including participants such as securities exchanges, broker-dealers, investment companies, and investment advisers—and takes enforcement actions against individuals and companies for violations of federal securities laws. SEC's mission is to protect investors; maintain fair, orderly, and efficient markets; and facilitate capital formation. Virtual currencies may have implications for a number of SEC responsibilities. For example, SEC has enforcement authority for violations of federal securities laws prohibiting fraud by any person in the purchase, offer, or sale of securities. SEC enforcement extends to virtual-currency-related securities transactions. Additionally, when companies offer and sell securities (including virtual-currency-related securities), they are subject to SEC requirements to either register the offering with SEC or qualify for a registration exemption. SEC reviews registration statements to ensure that potential investors receive adequate information about the issuer, the security, and the offering. Further, if a registered national securities exchange wanted to list a virtual-currency-related security, it could only do so if the listing complied with the exchange's existing rules or the exchange had filed a proposed rule change with SEC to permit the listing.

Virtual currencies may also have implications for other SEC responsibilities, as the following examples illustrate:

- SEC has examination authority for entities it regulates, including registered broker-dealers, to ensure compliance with federal securities laws, SEC rules and regulations, and BSA requirements. According to SEC officials, if a broker-dealer were to accept payments in virtual currencies from customers, this could raise potential anti-money-laundering issues that the broker-dealer would have to account for.
- SEC also regulates and has examination authority over investment advisers subject to its jurisdiction.[39] Under the Investment Advisers Act of 1940, investment advisers are fiduciaries.[40] To the extent that an investment adviser recommends virtual currencies or virtual-currency-related securities, the investment adviser's federal fiduciary duty would govern this conduct.
- If registered broker-dealers held virtual currencies for their own account or an account of a customer, SEC would have to determine how to treat the virtual currencies for purposes of its broker-dealer financial responsibility rules, including the net capital rule.[41]

Commodity Futures Trading Commission

CFTC has the authority to regulate financial derivative products and their markets, including commodity futures and options.[42] In addition, CFTC investigates and prosecutes alleged violations of the Commodity Exchange Act and related regulations.[43] CFTC's mission is to protect market users and the public from fraud, manipulation, abusive practices, and systemic risk related to derivatives subject to the Commodity Exchange Act. CFTC's responsibilities with respect to virtual currencies depend partly on whether bitcoin or other virtual currencies meet the definition of a commodity under the Commodity Exchange Act.[44] CFTC officials said the agency would not make a formal determination on this issue until market circumstances require one. According to CFTC, such circumstances could include virtual-currency derivatives emerging or being offered in the United States or CFTC becoming aware of the existence of fraud or manipulative schemes involving virtual currencies. The officials said that if prospective derivatives that are backed by or denominated in virtual currencies that CFTC determines to be commodities emerge, CFTC's regulatory authorities would apply to those derivatives just as they would for any other derivative product subject to CFTC's jurisdiction. To carry out its regulatory responsibilities, CFTC would, among other things, evaluate the derivatives to ensure they were not susceptible to manipulation, review applications for new exchanges wishing to offer such derivatives, and examine exchanges offering these derivatives to ensure compliance with the applicable commodity exchange laws.

Similar to SEC, CFTC has examination authority for BSA compliance—in this case directed at futures commission merchants and other futures market intermediaries—and acceptance of virtual currency payments by these entities could raise BSA compliance concerns.[45] Like SEC, CFTC would also have to make determinations about the capital treatment of virtual currencies if these entities held virtual currencies for their own account or an account of a customer.

Departments of Homeland Security and Justice

Law enforcement agencies, including but not limited to DHS and DOJ component agencies and offices, have responsibilities to investigate a variety of federal crimes that may involve the use of virtual currencies and to support the prosecution of those who commit these crimes. Like traditional currencies, virtual currencies can facilitate a range of criminal activities, including fraud schemes and the sale of illicit goods and services, that may fall under the purview of federal law enforcement agencies.

The emergence of virtual currencies has had particular significance for financial crimes. According to DOJ officials, the main law enforcement interests with respect to virtual currencies are to (1) deter and prosecute criminals who use virtual currency systems to launder money (that is, move or hide money that either facilitates or is derived from criminal or terrorist activities); and (2) investigate and prosecute virtual currency services that themselves violate money transmission and money laundering laws.[46] A number of DOJ and DHS components, including the FBI, ICE-HSI, and Secret Service, investigate financial crimes as part of their broader responsibilities. In addition, DOJ's Asset Forfeiture and Money Laundering Section prosecutes money laundering violations, and DOJ and DHS manage the seizure and forfeiture of assets that represent the proceeds of, or were used to facilitate, federal crimes. Key laws that may apply to the use of virtual currencies in financial crimes include BSA, as amended by Title III of the USA PATRIOT Act, and anti-money-laundering statutes.[47] Additionally, because virtual currencies operate over the Internet, they have implications for agency components that investigate and prosecute computer crimes (also called cybercrimes). For example, DOJ's Computer Crime and Intellectual Property Section stated that virtual currencies can be attractive to entities that seek to facilitate or conduct computer crimes over the Internet, such as computer-based fraud and identity theft. The section's responsibilities include improving legal processes for obtaining electronic evidence and working with other law enforcement agencies in improving the technological and operational means for gathering and analyzing electronic evidence. The FBI, Secret Service, and ICE-HSI also investigate computer crimes.

Virtual Currencies Present Regulatory, Law Enforcement, and Consumer Protection Challenges

The emergence of virtual currencies presents challenges to federal agencies responsible for financial regulation, law enforcement, and consumer and investor protection. These challenges stem partly from certain characteristics of virtual currencies, such as the higher degree of anonymity they provide and the ease with which they can be sent across borders. In addition, the growing popularity of virtual currencies has highlighted both risks and benefits for agencies to consider in carrying out their responsibilities.

Greater Anonymity

As previously noted, some virtual currency systems may provide a higher degree of anonymity than traditional payment systems because they do not require the disclosure of personally identifiable information (that is, information that can be used to locate or identify an individual, such as names or Social Security numbers) to transfer funds from one party to another. When transferring funds in the amount of $3,000 or more between the bank accounts of two individuals, the banks involved are required by FinCEN regulations to obtain and keep the names and other information of the individuals, as well as information on the transaction itself.[48] The customer identification information collected by the banks helps create a paper trail of financial transactions that law enforcement agencies can use to detect illegal activity, such as money laundering or terrorist financing, and to identify and apprehend criminals.[49] However, in a transfer between two individuals using bitcoins (or a similar type of decentralized virtual currency) no personally identifiable information is necessarily disclosed either to the two individuals or a third-party intermediary.[50] As a result, virtual currencies may be attractive to parties seeking to protect personally identifiable information, maintain financial privacy, buy or sell illicit goods and services, or move or conceal money obtained by illegal means. Further, virtual currency exchangers or administrators may be used to facilitate money laundering if they do not collect identifying information from customers and retain other transaction information.

For these reasons, law enforcement and federal financial regulatory agencies have indicated that virtual currencies can create challenges for agencies in detecting unlawful actions and the entities that carry them out. For example, the FBI has noted that because bitcoin does not have a centralized entity to monitor and report suspicious activity and process legal requests such as subpoenas, law enforcement agencies face difficulty in detecting suspicious transactions using bitcoins and identifying parties involved in these transactions.

Cross-Jurisdictional Nature

Because they operate over the Internet, virtual currencies can be used globally to make payments and funds transfers across borders. In addition, according to agency officials, many of the entities that exchange traditional currencies for virtual currencies (or vice versa) are located outside of the United States. If these exchangers have customers located in the United States, they must comply with BSA and anti-money-laundering requirements. Due to the cross-jurisdictional nature of virtual currency systems, federal financial regulatory and law enforcement agencies face challenges in enforcing these requirements and investigating and prosecuting transnational crimes that may involve virtual currencies.

For example, law enforcement may have to rely upon cooperation from international partners to conduct investigations, make arrests, and seize criminal assets. Additionally, violators, victims, and witnesses may reside outside of the United States, and relevant customer and transaction records may be held by entities in different jurisdictions, making it difficult for law enforcement and financial regulators to access them. Further, virtual currency exchangers or administrators may operate out of countries that have weak legal and regulatory regimes or that are less willing to cooperate with U.S. law enforcement.

Balancing Risks and Benefits

Virtual currency industry stakeholders have noted that virtual currencies present both risks and benefits that federal agencies need to consider in regulating entities that may be associated with virtual-currency-related activities. As previously noted, the risks include the attractiveness of virtual currencies to those who may want to launder money or purchase illicit goods and services. Another emerging set of risks involves consumer and investor protection—in particular, whether consumers and investors understand the potential drawbacks of buying, holding, and using virtual currencies or investing in virtual-currency-based securities. Consumers may not be aware of certain characteristics and risks of virtual currencies, including the following:

- *Lack of bank involvement.* Virtual currency exchanges and wallet providers are not banks. If they go out of business, there may be no specific protections like deposit insurance to cover consumer losses.[51]
- *Stated limits on financial recourse.* Some virtual currency wallet providers purport to disclaim responsibility for consumer losses associated with unauthorized wallet access. In contrast, credit and debit card networks state that consumers have no liability for fraudulent use of accounts.
- *Volatile prices.* The prices of virtual currencies can change quickly and dramatically (as shown previously in figure 2).

Additionally, an SEC official told us that virtual-currency-based securities may be attracting individuals who are younger and less experienced than typical investors. The official expressed concern that younger investors may lack the sophistication to properly assess the risks of such investments and the financial resources to recover from losses on the investments, including losses resulting from fraud schemes.[52] While virtual currencies present risks to consumers and investors, they also provide several potential benefits to consumers and business.

- *Cost and speed.* Decentralized virtual currency systems may, in some circumstances, provide lower transaction costs and be faster than traditional funds transfer systems because the transactions do not need to go through a third-party intermediary. The irrevocable feature of virtual currency payments may also contribute to lower transaction costs by eliminating the costs of consumer chargebacks.[53] Industry stakeholders have noted that cost and time savings may be especially significant for international remittances (personal funds immigrants send to their home countries), which sometimes involve sizeable fees and can take several days.

In addition, industry stakeholders have indicated that the potentially lower costs of virtual currency transactions—for example, relative to credit and debit cards—may facilitate the use of micropayments (very small financial transactions) as a way of selling items such as online news articles, music, and smartphone applications.

- *Financial privacy.* To the extent that bitcoin (or other virtual currency) addresses are not publicly associated with a specific individual, peer-to-peer virtual currency transactions can provide a greater degree of financial privacy than transactions using traditional payment systems, because no personally identifiable information is exchanged.[54]
- *Access.* Because virtual currencies can be accessed anywhere over the Internet, they are a potential way to provide basic financial services to populations without access to traditional financial institutions, such as rural populations in developing countries.[55] However, the potential benefit hinges on access to the Internet, which these populations may not have, and may be offset by the lack of protections against losses noted previously.

Federal agency officials have acknowledged the need to consider both the risks and benefits of virtual currencies in carrying out their responsibilities. For example, the Director of FinCEN has testified that the emergence of virtual currencies has prompted consideration of vulnerabilities that these currencies create in the financial system and how illicit actors will take advantage of them.

However, she also noted that innovation is an important part of the economy and that FinCEN needs to have regulation that mitigates concerns about illicit actors while minimizing regulatory burden. Similarly, the former Acting Assistant Attorney General for DOJ's Criminal Division has testified that law enforcement needs to be vigilant about the criminal misuse of virtual currency systems while recognizing that there are many legitimate users of those services.

Balancing concerns about the illicit use of virtual currencies against the potential benefits of these technological innovations will likely be an ongoing challenge for federal agencies.

Agencies Have Taken Some Actions on Virtual Currencies, but Interagency Working Groups Have Not Focused on Consumer Risks

Federal financial regulators and law enforcement agencies have taken a number of actions related to the emergence of virtual currencies, including providing regulatory guidance, assessing anti-money-laundering compliance, and investigating crimes and violations that have been facilitated by the use of virtual currencies. However, interagency working groups addressing virtual currencies have not focused on consumer protection and have generally not included CFPB.

FinCEN Has Issued Rules, Guidance, and Administrative Rulings Regarding Virtual Currencies

FinCEN has taken a number of actions in recent years to establish and clarify requirements for participants in virtual currency systems. For example, in July 2011, FinCEN finalized a rule that modified the definitions of certain money services businesses.[56] Among other things, the rule states that persons who accept and transmit currency, funds, or "other value that substitutes for currency," are considered to be money transmitters.[57] Additionally, in March 2013, FinCEN issued guidance that clarified the applicability of BSA regulations to participants in certain virtual currency systems.[58] The FinCEN guidance classified virtual currency exchangers and administrators as money services businesses and, more specifically, as money transmitters.[59] The guidance also specified that virtual currency users are not money services businesses.[60] As a result, the guidance clarified that virtual currency exchangers and administrators must follow requirements to register with FinCEN as money transmitters; institute risk assessment procedures and anti-money-laundering program control measures; and implement certain recordkeeping, reporting, and transaction monitoring requirements, unless an exception to these requirements applies.[61] According to FinCEN officials, as of December 2013, approximately 40 virtual currency exchangers or administrators had registered with FinCEN.

In 2014, in response to questions from industry stakeholders, FinCEN issued administrative rulings to clarify the types of participants to which the March 2013 guidance applies.[62] In January 2014, FinCEN issued rulings stating that the way in which a virtual currency is obtained is not material, but the way in which a person or corporation uses the virtual currency is. As a result, the rulings specify that two kinds of users are not considered money transmitters subject to FinCEN's regulations: miners who use and convert virtual currencies exclusively for their own purposes and companies that invest in virtual currencies exclusively as an investment for their own account.[63] However, the rulings specify that these two kinds of users may no longer be exempt from FinCEN's money transmitter requirements if they conduct their activities as a business service for others. The rulings also note that transfers of virtual currencies from these types of users to third parties should be closely scrutinized because they may constitute money transmission. In April 2014, FinCEN issued another administrative ruling, which states that companies that rent computer systems for mining virtual currencies are not considered money transmitters subject to FinCEN's regulations.[64]

FinCEN has also taken additional steps to help ensure that companies required to register as money services businesses under FinCEN's March 2013 virtual currency guidance have done so. According to FinCEN officials, FinCEN has responded to letters from companies seeking clarification about their requirements. Also, officials told us that FinCEN has proactively informed other companies that they should register as money services businesses.

Some Financial Regulators Have Taken Actions Concerning Anti-Money-Laundering and Securities Law Compliance

As part of their oversight activities, NCUA and SEC have addressed situations involving virtual currencies, and other federal financial regulators have had internal discussions regarding virtual currencies. NCUA has had two supervisory situations in which credit unions were involved with activity related to virtual currencies. These situations emerged after reviews of credit unions found that their anti-money-laundering and antifraud measures needed to be revised in light of activity involving virtual currency exchanges.

- In 2013, NCUA issued a preliminary warning letter to a federal credit union that provided account services to money services businesses that also served as bitcoin exchanges. The warning letter was based on various conditions that NCUA determined could undermine the credit union's stability. For example, the credit union did not have adequate anti-money-laundering controls in place for its money services business accounts. Further, the letter stated that the credit union should not have served money services businesses that were not part of the credit union's strategic plan, and that serving these businesses was not consistent with the credit union's charter, which called for serving the local community. The warning letter required the credit union to immediately cease all transactions with these money services business accounts and establish an appropriate BSA and anti-money-laundering infrastructure. As a result, the credit union ceased such activity and strengthened its BSA and anti-money-laundering compliance program.
- In 2012, NCUA provided support to a state regulator's review of a credit union's commercial customer. The state regulator found that this commercial customer was a payment processor—that is, a payment network that allows any business or person to send, request, and accept money—that had customers that were bitcoin exchanges. According to NCUA, the state regulator worked with the credit union to ensure that its BSA compliance program was adequate to monitor and address the risks associated with payment processors that serve bitcoin exchanges. The state regulator also worked to ensure that the payment processor's risk management practices included sufficient antifraud and anti-money-laundering measures. The payment processor subsequently suspended all accounts that served virtual currency exchanges.

In addition, SEC has taken enforcement action against an individual and entity that are alleged to have defrauded investors through a bitcoin-denominated Ponzi scheme.[65] The agency has also issued related investor alerts, has begun to review a registration statement from an entity that wants to offer virtual-currency-related securities, and is monitoring for potential securities law violations related to virtual currencies.

- In July 2013, SEC charged an individual and his company, Bitcoin Savings and Trust, with offering and selling securities in violation of the antifraud and registration provisions of securities laws.[66] Specifically, SEC alleges that the founder and operator defrauded investors through a bitcoin-denominated Ponzi scheme. The founder and operator allegedly promised investors up to 7 percent weekly interest. However, he allegedly used bitcoins from new investors to make purported interest payments and cover investor withdrawals on outstanding trust investments, diverted investors' bitcoins for day trading in his personal account on a bitcoin currency exchange, and exchanged investors' bitcoins for U.S. dollars to pay for personal expenses. SEC also alleges that Bitcoin Savings and Trust raised at least 700,000 bitcoins in investor funds, which amounted to more than $4.5 million based on the average price of bitcoin in 2011 and 2012 when the investments were offered and sold. This case was still unresolved as of April 14, 2014.

- SEC's Office of Investor Education and Advocacy has issued two investor alerts on virtual currencies.[67] The first alert, issued in July 2013, warned about fraudulent investment schemes that may involve bitcoin and other virtual currencies.[68] The second alert, issued in May 2014, addressed fraud and other investment risks related to virtual currencies.[69]
- SEC staff have begun to review a registration statement from a company that wants to conduct a public offering of virtual-currency-related securities and has received notice of a company offering a private virtual-currency-related security, relying upon an exemption from registration. In July 2013, the Winklevoss Bitcoin Trust filed a registration statement for an initial public offering of its securities. The Trust is structured similarly to an exchange-traded fund and will hold bitcoins as its only assets.[70] The Trust filed amended registration statements in October 2013 and February 2014, but the registration statement remains pending as of April 14, 2014, meaning that the Trust is not yet permitted to sell its securities in a public offering. Also, in October 2013, Bitcoin Investment Trust, a bitcoin-denominated pooled investment fund affiliated with SecondMarket, Inc. and available only to accredited investors, filed a notice with SEC indicating that it had sold securities in an exempt offering in reliance on Rule 506(c) of the Securities Act.[71] Rule 506(c) allows an issuer to raise an unlimited amount of money, but imposes restrictions on who can invest in the offering and requires the issuer to take reasonable steps to verify that those investing are accredited investors.[72]

- SEC staff are also monitoring the Internet and other sources, such as referrals from other agencies, for potential securities law violations involving bitcoin and other virtual currencies.

Further, all of the federal financial regulatory agencies we interviewed have had internal discussions on how virtual currencies work and what implications the emergence of virtual currencies might have for their responsibilities. While agencies generally told us that their conversations have been informal and ad hoc, some efforts have been more organized:

- In 2013, the Federal Reserve took several steps to share information on virtual currencies among the Board of Governors and the 12 Federal Reserve Banks. Among other things, the Board of Governors' BSA and anti-money-laundering specialist conference included a session focused on FinCEN's virtual currency guidance and recent law enforcement actions. The Board of Governors also circulated general information about virtual currencies within the Federal Reserve System to use in answering questions from media and the public about virtual currencies and federal financial regulatory actions to date.
- In 2013, SEC formed an internal Digital Currency Working Group, which aims to foster information sharing internally and externally. According to SEC, the working group consists of approximately 50 members from among SEC's divisions and offices.
- In 2012, FinCEN held three internal information-sharing events on virtual currencies. These events covered issues including how virtual currencies compare to traditional currencies and risks related to emerging payment systems such as virtual currencies.

Law Enforcement Agencies Have Taken Actions against Parties Alleged to Have Used Virtual Currencies to Facilitate Crimes

Law enforcement agencies have taken actions against parties involved in the illicit use of virtual currencies to facilitate crimes. These parties have included administrators and users of centralized virtual currency systems designed to facilitate money laundering or other crimes, parties who have used virtual currencies to buy or sell illicit goods and services online, and virtual currency exchanges and online payment processors operating without the proper licenses.

- In 2013 and 2014, law enforcement agencies took actions against Silk Road, a black market website that allegedly accepted bitcoin as the sole payment method for the purchase of illegal goods and services. The website contained over 13,000 listings for controlled substances as well as listings for malicious software programs, pirated media content, fake passports, and computer hacking services (see figure 3). The FBI; Drug Enforcement Administration (DEA); IRS; ICE-HSI; the Bureau of Alcohol, Tobacco, Firearms, and Explosives; the Secret Service; the U.S. Marshals Service; and Treasury's Office of Foreign Assets Control investigated the case together, along with officials from New York as well as Australia, Iceland, Ireland, and France. In September and October 2013, law enforcement shut down the Silk Road website and seized approximately 174,000 bitcoins, which the FBI reported were worth approximately $34 million at the time of seizure.[73] In February 2014, DOJ indicted Silk Road's alleged owner and operator on charges including narcotics conspiracy, engaging in a continuing criminal enterprise, conspiracy to commit computer hacking, and money laundering conspiracy.

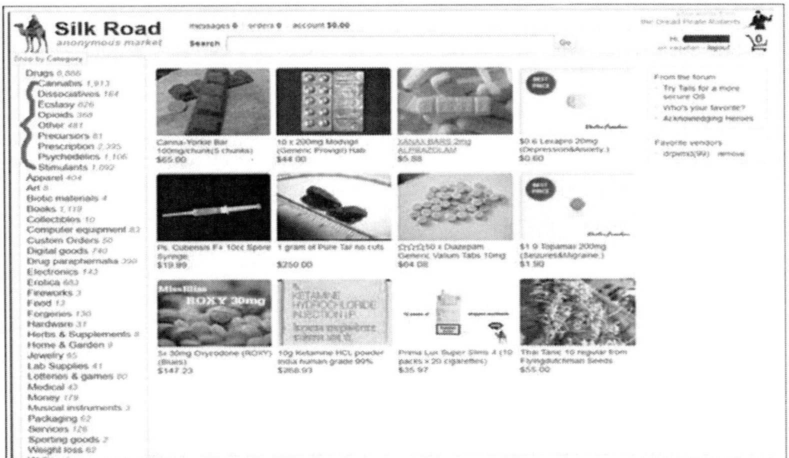

Source: U.S. Immigation and Customs Enforcement.

Figure 3. Screen Shot of the Silk Road Website.

- In May 2013, law enforcement agencies seized the accounts of a U.S.-based subsidiary of Mt. Gox, a now-defunct Tokyo-based virtual currency exchange with users from multiple countries including the United States, on the basis that the subsidiary was operating as an unlicensed money services business. The seizure included U.S. bank accounts of Mt. Gox that were held by a private bank and Dwolla, an online payment processor that allegedly allowed users to buy and sell bitcoins on Mt. Gox.

  According to ICE-HSI, Mt. Gox had moved funds into numerous online black markets, the bulk of which were associated with the illicit purchase of drugs, firearms, and child pornography. At the direction of the U.S. Attorney's office, ICE-HSI ordered Dwolla to stop all payments to Mt. Gox and seized $5.1 million from the Mt. Gox subsidiary's U.S. accounts.
- Also in May 2013, law enforcement agencies shut down Liberty Reserve, a centralized virtual currency system that was allegedly designed and frequently used to facilitate money laundering and had its own virtual currency. Secret Service, ICE-HSI, and IRS investigated the case together, along with officials from 16 other countries. To shut down the site, FinCEN identified Liberty Reserve as a financial institution of primary money laundering concern under section 311 of the USA PATRIOT Act, effectively cutting it off from the U.S. financial system.[74] DOJ then charged Liberty Reserve with operating an unlicensed money transmission business and with money laundering for facilitating the movement of more than $6 billion in illicit proceeds.[75]

  As of April 2014, this investigation had produced $40 million in seizures and had resulted in the arrests of five individuals.
- In April 2013, law enforcement agencies filed a civil asset forfeiture complaint against Tcash Ads Inc., an online payment processor that allegedly enabled users to make purchases anonymously from virtual currency exchanges, with operating an unlicensed money services business.

  Additionally, law enforcement agencies seized the bank accounts of Tcash Ads Inc. The Secret Service worked on the case with FinCEN and DOJ's Asset Forfeiture and Money Laundering Section.
- From October 2010 through November 2012, law enforcement agencies convicted three organizers of a worldwide conspiracy to use a network of virus-controlled computers that deployed e-mail spam

designed to manipulate stock prices. The organizers paid the spammers $1.4 million for their illegal services via the centralized virtual currency e-Gold and wire transfers. Charges included conspiring to further securities fraud using spam, conspiring to transmit spam through unauthorized access to computers, and four counts of transmission of spam by unauthorized computers.

Law enforcement agencies have also taken other actions to help support investigations involving the illicit use of virtual currencies, including the following examples.

- The FBI has produced numerous criminal intelligence products addressing virtual currencies. These intelligence products have generally focused on cases involving the illicit use of virtual currencies, ways in which virtual currencies have been or could be used to facilitate crimes, and the related challenges for law enforcement. The FBI shares these products with foreign, state, and local law enforcement partners as appropriate.
- Through standing bilateral agreements governing the exchange of law enforcement information, ICE-HSI is arranging meetings with various international partners to exchange intelligence and garner operational support on virtual currency issues.
- ICE-HSI also developed the Illicit Digital Economy Program, which aims to target the use of virtual currencies for money-laundering purposes by defining and organizing the primary facets of the digital economy, building internal capacity, training and developing agents and analysts, engaging other agencies, and promoting public-private partnerships.

Interagency Working Groups Have Begun to Address Virtual Currencies, but Have Not Emphasized Consumer Risks or Generally Included CFPB

Federal agency efforts to collaborate on virtual currency issues have involved creating a working group specifically focused on virtual currency, leveraging existing interagency mechanisms, and sharing information through informal interagency channels.

For example, in 2012, the FBI formed the Virtual Currency Emerging Threats Working Group (VCET), an interagency working group that includes other DOJ components, FinCEN, ICE-HSI, SEC, Secret Service, Treasury, and other relevant federal partners. The purpose of VCET is to leverage members' expertise to address new virtual currency trends, address potential implications for law enforcement and the U.S. intelligence community, and mitigate the cross-programmatic threats arising from illicit actors' use of virtual currency systems. The VCET meets about once every 3 months.

Federal agencies have also begun to discuss virtual currency issues in existing interagency working groups that address broader topics such as money laundering, electronic crimes, and the digital economy, as follows:

- The BSA Advisory Group—which is chaired by FinCEN and includes the prudential banking regulators, Treasury, federal and state law enforcement and regulatory agencies, and industry representatives—has addressed virtual currency issues in a number of ways. In May 2013, FinCEN provided a briefing on bitcoin, and in December 2013 three stakeholders from the virtual currency industry gave presentations on their business models and regulatory challenges. In addition, the BSA Advisory Group invited a representative of the virtual currency industry to join the group in 2014.
- The Federal Financial Institutions Examination Council (FFIEC) Bank Secrecy Act/Anti-Money-Laundering Working Group—which is currently chaired by OCC and includes the prudential banking regulators and CFPB—is in the process of revising the current (2010) FFIEC BSA/Anti-Money Laundering Examination Manual.[76] The revisions related to virtual currencies may include information on FinCEN's March 2013 guidance and regulatory expectations that depository institutions should undertake a risk assessment with a particular focus on the money laundering risks posed by new products and services.
- The Secret Service-sponsored Electronic Crimes Task Forces (ECTF) includes 35 Secret Service field offices; federal law enforcement agencies such as ICE-HSI; and members of the private sector, academia, and state and local law enforcement.[77] This group's mission is to prevent, detect, and investigate electronic crimes, including those involving virtual currency. This group has conducted computer forensics and other investigative activity on various virtual currencies and made arrests of individuals who have used virtual currencies as

part of their criminal activities. This group has also held quarterly meetings on virtual currencies to discuss legal and regulatory issues and trends in crimes involving virtual currencies.

- The Digital Economy Task Force was established in 2013 by Thomson Reuters (a multinational media and information firm) and the International Centre for Missing & Exploited Children.[78] This task force includes members from both the public and private sectors. Task force members from the federal government include representatives from the FBI, ICE-HSI, Secret Service, the Department of State, and the United States Agency for International Development. This group published a report in March 2014 on the benefits and challenges of the digital economy.[79] Among other things, the report recommended continuing private and public research into the digital economy and illegal activities, investing in law enforcement training, rethinking investigative techniques, fostering cooperation between agencies, and promoting a national and global dialogue on policy related to virtual currencies.

A number of other existing interagency working groups have discussed or addressed virtual currency issues to some extent. See appendix II for more information on these groups.

Federal agencies have also started to collaborate outside of these working groups to help improve their knowledge of issues related to the emergence of virtual currencies and share pertinent information with various agencies.

- FinCEN and SEC have hosted meetings with industry representatives and consultants to discuss how virtual currency systems such as bitcoin and Ripple work and what legal, regulatory, technology, and law enforcement issues they present. These agencies have invited officials from other federal agencies to these sessions.
- FinCEN consulted with financial regulators and law enforcement agencies as it was formulating its March 2013 guidance on virtual currencies. These agencies included CFPB, CFTC, DEA, FBI, ICE-HSI, IRS, the prudential banking regulators, SEC, and the Secret Service.
- SEC notified CFTC of its review of the Winklevoss Bitcoin Trust registration statement.
- FinCEN issued a Networking Bulletin on cryptocurrencies in March 2013 to provide details to law enforcement agencies and assist them in

following money moving between virtual currency channels and the traditional U.S. financial system. Among other things, the bulletin addressed the role of entities that facilitate the purchase and exchange of virtual currencies and the types of records these entities maintain that could be useful to investigative officials. Also, the Networking Bulletin elicited information from its recipients, which in turn helped FinCEN issue additional analytical products of a tactical nature to inform law enforcement operations. FinCEN has also shared this information with several regulatory and foreign financial intelligence unit partners.

- CFPB officials said they had recently conferred on virtual currency issues with a number of domestic and international regulators, including the Federal Reserve Bank of San Francisco, the Federal Trade Commission, NCUA, OCC, Treasury, New York State's Department of Financial Services, and the European Banking Authority. In addition, the officials said they had met with industry participants on these issues and conferred with interested academic and consumer group stakeholders, as well as law firms, consultancies, and industry associations.

Although there are numerous interagency collaborative efforts that have addressed virtual currency issues in some manner, interagency working groups have not focused on consumer protection issues. Rather, as previously discussed, these efforts have focused on BSA and anti-money-laundering controls and investigations of crimes in which virtual currencies have been used.

In addition, CFPB's involvement in interagency working groups that address virtual currencies has been limited. GAO's key practices on collaboration state that it is important to include relevant participants in interagency collaborative efforts in order to ensure, among other things, that these participants contribute knowledge, skills, and abilities to the outcomes of the effort.[80]

In addition, these key practices state that once an interagency group has been established, it is important to reach out to potential participants who may have a shared interest in order to ensure that opportunities for achieving outcomes are not missed.[81] CFPB might be a relevant participant in a broader set of collaborative efforts on virtual currencies because virtual currency systems provide a new way of making financial transactions, and CFPB's responsibilities include ensuring that consumers have timely and understandable information to make responsible decisions about financial transactions.[82] Further, CFPB's strategic goals include helping consumers understand the costs, risks, and tradeoffs of financial decisions and surfacing financial trends and emergent risks relevant to consumers.

Although interagency working groups addressing virtual currencies have not focused on consumer protection issues, recent events have highlighted the risks individuals face in buying and holding these currencies. For example, notable examples of bitcoin thefts by computer hackers have occurred in the past few years, including the theft of more than 35,000 bitcoins from a virtual wallet provider in April 2013 and 24,000 bitcoins from a bitcoin exchange in September 2012.[83]

More recently, in February 2014, Mt. Gox filed for bankruptcy, stating that a security breach resulted in the loss of 850,000 bitcoins, the vast majority of which belonged to its customers. These bitcoins were worth more than $460 million when Mt. Gox filed for bankruptcy.[84] Mt. Gox subsequently reported that it had found 200,000 of these bitcoins in an unused virtual wallet.

Certain parties have taken actions to inform consumers about the potential risks associated with virtual currencies, but these actions have occurred outside of federal interagency efforts and have not included CFPB. In April 2014, the Conference of State Bank Supervisors and the North American Securities Administrators Association issued joint model consumer guidance to assist state regulatory agencies in educating consumers about virtual currencies and the risks of purchasing, exchanging, and investing in virtual currencies.[85]

Additionally, from February through April 2014, a number of states issued consumer alerts about virtual currencies.[86] On the international front, the European Banking Authority issued a warning to consumers in December 2013 about the risks involved in buying or holding virtual currencies.[87]

Federal interagency working groups addressing virtual currency issues have not focused on consumer protection, and CFPB has generally not participated in these groups, for a number of potential reasons. For example, the extent to which individuals using virtual currencies are speculative investors or ordinary consumers is unclear, and CFPB has received few consumer complaints about these currencies.[88] In addition, incidents involving the use of virtual currencies for illicit purposes have made money laundering and other law enforcement issues primary concerns, and existing interagency working groups are primarily composed of agencies that share responsibilities for these matters.

However, emerging consumer risks indicate that interagency collaborative efforts may need to place greater emphasis on consumer protection issues in order to address the full range of challenges posed by virtual currencies. Additionally, without CFPB's participation, interagency working groups are not fully leveraging the expertise of the lead consumer financial protection agency, and CFPB may not be receiving information that it could use to assess the risks that virtual currencies pose to consumers.

CONCLUSION

Bitcoin and other virtual currencies are technological innovations that provide users with certain benefits but also pose a number of risks. Because virtual currencies touch on the responsibilities of multiple federal agencies, addressing these risks will require effective interagency collaboration. Thus far, interagency efforts have had a law enforcement focus, reflecting the attractiveness of virtual currencies to those who may want to launder money or purchase black market items. If virtual currencies become more widely used, other types of regulatory and enforcement issues may come to the forefront. For example, recent events suggest that consumer protection is an emerging risk, as evidenced by the loss or theft of bitcoins from exchanges and virtual wallet providers and consumer warnings issued by nonfederal and non-U.S. entities.

However, federal interagency working groups addressing virtual currencies have thus far not emphasized consumer-protection issues, and participation by the federal government's lead consumer financial protection agency, CFPB, has been limited.

Therefore, these efforts may not be consistent with key practices that can benefit interagency collaboration, such as including all relevant participants to ensure that their knowledge, skills, and abilities contribute to the outcomes of the effort.

As a result, future interagency efforts may not be in a position to address consumer risks associated with virtual currencies in the most timely and effective manner.

RECOMMENDATION FOR EXECUTIVE ACTION

To help ensure that federal interagency collaboration on virtual currencies addresses emerging consumer protection issues, we recommend that the Director of CFPB (1) identify which interagency working groups could help CFPB maintain awareness of these issues or would benefit from CFPB's participation; and (2) decide, in coordination with the agencies already participating in these efforts, which ones CFPB should participate in.

AGENCY COMMENTS

We provided a draft of this report to CFPB, CFTC, DOJ, DHS, FDIC, the Federal Reserve, NCUA, OCC, SEC, and Treasury for review and comment. CFPB and NCUA provided written comments. In addition, CFPB, CFTC, DHS, DOJ, the Federal Reserve, NCUA, OCC, SEC, and Treasury provided technical comments, which we incorporated into the report where appropriate.

In its letter, CFPB concurred with our recommendation to identify and participate in pertinent interagency working groups addressing virtual currencies. CFPB stated that, to date, these groups have primarily focused on BSA concerns, anti-money-laundering controls, and the investigation of crimes involving virtual currencies. CFPB said that, as a result, its participation in these working groups has been limited. CFPB also stated that as consumer protection concerns have increased in recent months, its own work on virtual currencies and the work of other financial regulators in this area could benefit from a collaborative approach.

In its letter, NCUA said that the report provides a clear discussion of the risks related to virtual currencies as well as a survey of current efforts in the regulatory community to address the related policy issues. NCUA also expressed support for increasing emphasis on consumer protection issues pertaining to virtual currencies.

Lawrance L. Evans, Jr.
Director,
Financial Markets and Community Investment

APPENDIX I. HOW BITCOINS CIRCULATION AND ARE USED ENTER INTO IN TRANSACTIONS

This appendix shows how bitcoins enter into circulation through "mining," how transactions are conducted, and how miners verify transactions (see figure 4).

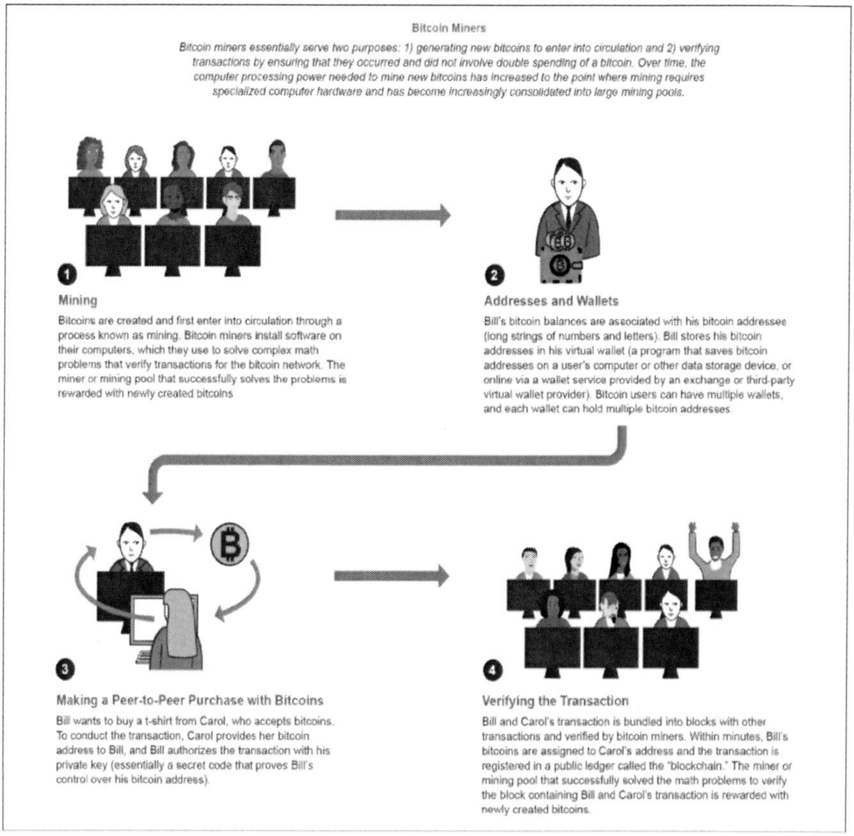

Source: GAO.

Figure 4. How Bitcoins Enter into Circulation and Are Used in Transactions.

APPENDIX II. INTERAGENCY WORKING GROUPS THAT HAVE ADDRESSED VIRTUAL CURRENCY ISSUES

In this appendix, we present some of the interagency working groups (including task forces and other interagency collaborative bodies) that have discussed virtual currency issues, and in some cases, taken specific actions. This list is based on information we obtained from the federal financial regulatory and law enforcement agencies we met with and is not intended to be an exhaustive list.

Table 1. Interagency Working Groups that Have Addressed Virtual Currency Issues, as of April 2014

Working group	Participating agencies	Mission and goals	Ways in which group addressed virtual currencies
Bank Secrecy Act Advisory Group (BSAAG)	FinCEN (lead); CFTC; DEA; DOJ Criminal Division; FBI; FDIC; Federal Reserve; ICE-HSI; IRS; NCUA; OCC; Office of National Drug Control Policy; SEC; Secret Service; and U.S. Postal Service; as well as representatives of financial institutions; trade groups; self-regulatory organizations; and state regulatory agencies.	This public-private group serves as a means by which the Secretary of the Treasury receives advice on the manner in which reporting requirements in BSA should be modified to enhance the ability of law enforcement agencies to use the information. It also informs private sector representatives of law enforcement's uses of BSA reports provided by financial institutions.	Meetings have covered issues related to virtual currencies: • The May 2013 meeting included a briefing on the bitcoin virtual currency system. • The December 2013 meeting included a panel of virtual currency industry representatives who discussed business models and regulatory compliance challenges. • In April 2014, a meeting of the BSAAG Illicit Finance Committee included a presentation on vulnerabilities and challenges related to virtual currencies, as well as

Table 1. (Continued)

Working group	Participating agencies	Mission and goals	Ways in which group addressed virtual currencies
			opportunities to enhance collective anti-money-laundering efforts and information sharing. In addition, BSAAG invited a representative of the virtual currency industry to join the group in 2014.
Digital Economy Task Force	Thomson Reuters and the International Centre for Missing & Exploited Children (lead); FBI; ICE-HSI; Secret Service; Department of State; and United States Agency for International Development (USAID); as well as members of the private sector and academia.	This group's mission is to educate the public, work collaboratively across stakeholder groups, and balance the convenience of the digital currencies with controls to combat illegal activity.	Created in September 2013, this task force has formed working groups on such issues as safeguarding human rights; regulation; interagency coordination; and law enforcement. In March 2014, the task force published a report on the benefits and challenges of the digital economy.[a] Among other things, the report recommended private and public sector efforts to continue research into the digital economy and illegal activities; investing in law enforcement training; rethinking investigative techniques; fostering cooperation between agencies; and promoting a national and global dialogue on policy.
Electronic Crimes Task Forces	35 Secret Service field offices (lead) and federal law	The mission of these groups is to prevent, detect, and	ECTFs address issues concerning virtual currencies as one of a variety

Working group	Participating agencies	Mission and goals	Ways in which group addressed virtual currencies
(ECTF) and Working Groups	enforcement agencies such as ICE-HSI, as well as members of the private sector, academia, and state and local law enforcement.	investigate various forms of electronic crime, including potential terrorist attacks against critical infrastructure and financial payment systems.	of subjects related to the investigations into electronic crime. Specifically, ECTFs have: • conducted computer forensics and other investigative activity concerning various virtual currencies; • made arrests of individuals who have used virtual currencies as part of their criminal activities; and • discussed virtual currencies at quarterly meetings, covering topics such as types of virtual currencies and related legal and regulatory issues, trends in criminal uses, and methods for conducting investigations.
Federal Financial Institutions Examination Council (FFIEC) BSA/Anti-Money-Laundering Working Group[b]	OCC (rotating chair), CFPB; FDIC; Federal Reserve; NCUA; and the State Liaison Committee are voting members.[c]	FFIEC prescribes uniform principles, standards, and report forms for the federal examination of financial institutions by the prudential banking regulators—FDIC, Federal Reserve, NCUA, and OCC—and makes recommendations to promote uniformity in the supervision of financial institutions. Within this context, the FFIEC	The BSA/Anti-Money-Laundering Working Group is leading the revision of the current (2010) FFIEC BSA/Anti-Money Laundering Examination Manual. Revisions related to virtual currencies may include information on FinCEN's March 2013 guidance; a brief note describing Internet-based electronic cash, which includes virtual currency; and regulatory expectations that banks should

Table 1. (Continued)

Working group	Participating agencies	Mission and goals	Ways in which group addressed virtual currencies
		BSA/Anti-Money-Laundering Working Group's mission is to enhance coordination of BSA/anti-money-laundering training, guidance, and policy.	undertake a risk assessment with a particular focus on the money-laundering risks posed by new products, services, and technologies.
Financial Action Task Force (FATF)	FATF is an international intergovernmental organization with 36 member countries, including the U.S. Treasury as the lead agency of the U.S. delegation. Other U.S. delegation participants include DOJ's Asset Forfeiture and Money Laundering Section; DHS (including ICE-HSI); SEC; IRS; and the Department of State.	This group sets standards and promotes effective implementation of legal, regulatory, and operational measures for combating money laundering, and the financing of terrorism and proliferation.	• In February 2014, FATF developed a discussion paper on virtual currencies, which described virtual currency systems, participants, and some of the major virtual currencies such as bitcoin, and proposed a common set of terms and conceptual framework for analyzing virtual currencies. The paper also discussed the potential legitimate uses of virtual currencies, the risks these currencies may pose, and the different regulatory approaches countries are taking to address virtual currencies. The U.S. delegation prepared the paper together with delegations from Australia, Canada, Russia, and the United Kingdom. As of April 2014, the discussion paper was not yet public.

Working group	Participating agencies	Mission and goals	Ways in which group addressed virtual currencies
			• In March 2014, FATF included a discussion of virtual currencies as part of the Private Sector Consultative Forum, which included experts on virtual currencies. The group discussed how virtual currencies and their exchangers operate; the associated money laundering and terrorist financing risks; what measures countries and financial institutions are taking to assess and mitigate those risks; and what regulatory approaches are currently being taken.
Interagency Bank Fraud Enforcement Working Group	DOJ (Criminal Division lead, as well as the Asset Forfeiture and Money Laundering Section, Executive Office for U.S. Attorneys, Executive Office for U.S. Trustees, and FBI); CFPB; CFTC; Department of Housing and Urban Development; DHS (ICE-HSI and Secret Service); Export-Import Bank; Farm Credit Administration; FDIC; Federal Housing Finance Agency; Federal Reserve; IRS;	This group's mission is to share information on significant trends, developments, and other issues in financial institution fraud and, as appropriate, identify and carry out projects of common interest to the working group's members.	The working group has occasionally discussed virtual currencies in the past year. Discussions to date have aimed to educate and inform members about virtual currencies. Planned activities include a presentation on the IRS notice addressing the status of virtual currencies under federal tax law. Within the Interagency Bank Fraud Working Group, the Payments Fraud Working Group has also addressed virtual currencies. The June 2013 meeting included presentations on e-

Table 1. (Continued)

Working group	Participating agencies	Mission and goals	Ways in which group addressed virtual currencies
	NCUA; OCC; SEC; Treasury (Bureau of Public Debt, FinCEN, Office of Inspector General, Office of General Counsel, Office of Critical Infrastructure Protection, Office of Financial Stability, and Special Inspector General for the Troubled Asset Relief Program); U.S. Postal Inspection Service; and the District of Columbia Department of Insurance, Securities, and Banking.		Gold, the Liberty Reserve indictment, and FinCEN's guidance on how BSA regulations apply to participants in certain virtual currency systems.
International Organized Crime Intelligence and Operations Center (IOC-2)	DOJ (lead, including the Bureau of Alcohol, Firearms and Explosives; Criminal Division, DEA, and FBI); DHS (ICE-HSI and Secret Service); IRS-Criminal Investigation; Department of Labor (Office of Inspector General); Department of State (Bureau of Diplomatic Security); and U.S. Postal Inspection Service.	This group's mission is to significantly disrupt and dismantle transnational criminal organizations posing the greatest threat to the United States. The group does so by (1) deconflicting and analyzing transnational organized crime information and intelligence; (2) disseminating information and intelligence to support law	IOC-2 supports member-agency investigations of both virtual currency administrators that are suspected of violating U.S. law and individuals who are suspected of using virtual currencies to commit crimes. Specifically, IOC-2 assists its member agencies by: • sharing investigative details that will serve to deconflict current investigative and prosecutorial targets;

Working group	Participating agencies	Mission and goals	Ways in which group addressed virtual currencies
		enforcement operations, investigations, prosecutions, and forfeiture proceedings; and (3) coordinating jurisdictional and multiagency operations, investigations and prosecutions.	• identifying current trends in the illicit use of virtual currencies; • sharing best practices in developing investigative and prosecutorial strategies; • discussing investigative challenges and solutions; • identifying tools, points of contact, and other areas of interest that offer assistance and serve as force multipliers in supporting virtual currency investigations and prosecutions; and • creating cross-agency relationships for future cooperation and coordination on virtual currency issues, investigations, and prosecutions.
Terrorist Finance Working Group's New Payments Systems Ad Hoc Working Group	Department of State (lead, including the Bureaus of Economic and Business Affairs, Counterterrorism, and International Narcotics and Law Enforcement Affairs); Department of Defense; DOJ (Asset Forfeiture and Money Laundering Section; Criminal Division; DEA; FBI; National	The larger working group's mission is to coordinate counter-terrorism-financing and anti-money-laundering training and technical assistance programs to countries deemed most vulnerable to terrorist financing. Within this context, the New Payments Ad Hoc Working	The New Payments Ad Hoc Working Group, which formed in 2013 and meets every two to three months, has addressed the use of virtual currencies at several meetings. Topics have included: • briefings on virtual currencies, how they operate, and risks; • the set of common virtual currency vocabulary terms proposed in the

Table 1. (Continued)

Working group	Participating agencies	Mission and goals	Ways in which group addressed virtual currencies
	Security Division; and Office of Overseas Prosecutorial Development, Assistance and Training); FDIC; Federal Trade Commission; ICE-HSI; IRS-Criminal Investigation; Treasury (FinCEN, Office of Terrorism and Financial Intelligence, and Office of Technical Assistance), and USAID.	Group's mission is two-fold: (1) to help ensure that foreign partners providing assistance and capacity building have a baseline understanding of new payment systems and the counter-terrorism-financing and anti-money-laundering risks and vulnerabilities that they may pose, and (2) to collaborate with other federal agencies and appropriate public and private sector entities to develop training and technical assistance programs in line with international standards set by groups such as FATF.	• FATF's discussion paper on virtual currencies; • trainings that ad hoc working group participants plan to offer through 2015 on counter-terrorism-financing and anti-money- laundering risks associated with virtual currencies. • workshops that the Department of State, USAID, and other ad hoc working group participants offered in 2013 and 2014 on new payment systems—including virtual currencies—to foreign partners in the East Africa, Southeast Asia, Latin America, and the Caribbean. • the ways in which other interagency collaborative groups—such as the Egmont Group, which is composed of FinCEN and financial intelligence units from other countries—are addressing virtual currencies.
Virtual Currencies Emerging Threats Working Group	DOJ (FBI lead and other DOJ components); FinCEN; ICE-HSI; SEC; Treasury; Secret	To address the illicit use of virtual currencies.	This group leverages members' expertise to address new virtual currency trends, address potential implications for law

Working group	Participating agencies	Mission and goals	Ways in which group addressed virtual currencies
	Service; and other relevant federal partners.		enforcement and the U.S. intelligence community, and mitigate the cross-programmatic threats arising from illicit actors' use of virtual currency systems.

Source: GAO analysis of agency interviews and documents, as well as websites of interagency collaborative efforts.

[a] Digital Economy Task Force, *The Digital Economy: Potential, Perils, and Promises* (Mar. 2014).

[b] FDIC, the Federal Reserve, and NCUA told us that the FFIEC Taskforce on Supervision, and the Taskforce's Information Technology Subgroup, have also discussed virtual currencies.

[c] The FFIEC State Liaison Committee includes representatives from the Conference of State Bank Supervisors, the American Council of State Savings Supervisors, and the National Association of State Credit Union Supervisors. Other FFIEC BSA/Anti-Money-Laundering Working Group non-voting members include CFTC; FinCEN; IRS; SEC; Treasury's Office of Foreign Assets Control; and Treasury's Office of Terrorist Financing and Financial Crimes.

End Notes

[1] Other federal agencies that were outside the scope of this report, such as the Internal Revenue Service (IRS), have responsibilities related to virtual currencies. For example, as we reported in May 2013, IRS is responsible for ensuring taxpayer compliance for all economic areas, including virtual economies and currencies. For more information, see GAO, *Virtual Economies and Currencies: Additional IRS Guidance Could Reduce Tax Compliance Risks*, GAO-13-516 (Washington, D.C.: May 15, 2013). In March 2014, IRS determined that virtual currencies will be treated as property for purposes of U.S. federal taxes. Therefore, general tax principles that apply to property transactions apply to transactions using virtual currency. See IRS Notice 2014-21.

[2] We reviewed testimony and agency statements from two congressional hearings: the November 18, 2013, U.S. Senate Committee on Homeland Security and Governmental Affairs hearing "Beyond Silk Road: Potential Risks, Threats, and Promises of Virtual Currencies," and the November 19, 2013, U.S. Senate Committee on Banking, Housing, and Urban Affairs hearing, "The Present and Future Impact of Virtual Currency."

[3] Pub. L. No. 91-508, 84 Stat. 1114 (1970) (codified as amended at 12 U.S.C. §§ 1829(b), 1951-1959; 31 U.S.C. §§ 5311-5330); Pub. L. No. 107-56, 115 Stat. 272 (2001) (codified as amended in scattered sections of U.S.C.).

[4] FinCEN, *Application of FinCEN's Regulations to Persons Administering, Exchanging, or Using Virtual Currencies*, FIN-2013-G001, March 18, 2013; FinCEN, *Application of FinCEN's Regulations to Virtual Currency Mining Operations*, FIN-2014-R001, January 30, 2014; FinCEN, *Application of FinCEN's Regulations to Virtual Currency Software Development and Certain Investment Activity*, FIN-2014-R002, January 30, 2014; and FinCEN, *Application of Money Services Business Regulations to the Rental of Computer Systems for Mining Virtual Currencies*, FIN-2014-R007, April 29, 2014.

[5] The Digital Economy Task Force was established in 2013 by Thomson Reuters (a multinational media and information firm) and the International Centre for Missing & Exploited Children to explore the benefits and risks of the emerging digital economy, including the use of virtual currency. This task force includes members from both the public and private sectors.

[6] GAO, *Managing for Results: Key Considerations for Implementing Interagency Collaborative Mechanisms*, GAO-12-1022 (Washington, D.C.: Sept. 27, 2012) and *Managing for Results: Implementation Approaches Used to Enhance Collaboration in Interagency Groups*, GAO-14-220 (Washington, D.C.: Feb. 14, 2014).

[7] GAO-13-516. In that report we described "closed-flow" virtual currencies as those that can be used only within a game or virtual environment and cannot be cashed out for dollars or other government-issued currencies. We also described hybrid virtual currencies as those that have characteristics of both open- and closed-flow currencies—for example, such currencies can be used to buy real goods and services but are not exchangeable for government-issued currencies.

[8] Some stakeholders with whom we spoke said they preferred the term digital currency to virtual currency, due partly to the connotation that something which is virtual cannot be used in the real world. We use the term virtual currency to be consistent with terminology used in prior GAO work and in key federal guidance on participants in virtual currency systems.

[9] A peer-to-peer network allows users to share data directly and conduct permitted activities without a central server.

[10] Cryptography is a branch of mathematics that is based on the transformation of data and can be used to provide security services such as confidentiality and authentication. Bitcoin and other virtual currencies that use cryptography are sometimes called cryptocurrencies.

[11] According to industry observers, examples of technologies used to increase the privacy of participants in virtual currency transactions include (1) anonymizing networks, which use a distributed network of computers to conceal the real Internet address of users, such as The

Onion Router (TOR); (2) "tumblers" such as BitcoinBath and BitLaundry that combine payments from multiple users to obstruct identification through the blockchain; and (3) alternative virtual currencies such as Zerocoin and Anoncoin that aim to make transactions fully anonymous.

[12] See Sarah Meiklejohn, et al, "A Fistful of Bitcoins: Characterizing Payments Among Men with No Names," *;Login:,* vol. 38 no. 6 (2013), available at https://www.usenix.org/system/files/login/articles/03_meiklejohn-online.pdf.

[13] By design, there will be a maximum of 21 million bitcoins in circulation once all bitcoins have been mined, which is projected to occur in the year 2140. Once all bitcoins have been mined, miners will be rewarded for solving the math problems that verify the validity of bitcoin transactions through fees rather than bitcoins.

[14] Given these limitations, we did not test the reliability of data, such as the data generated from the bitcoin network, but we are providing some figures to provide context for the possible size of the bitcoin market and other virtual currency markets.

[15] http://blockchain.info. (Accessed on Mar. 31, 2014.) Due to data limitations, it is difficult to calculate the velocity, or the rate at which bitcoins are spent, and the number of transactions between unique users in a given time period.

[16] For data on bitcoin price, see https://www.coindesk.com. (Accessed on Apr. 1, 2014.) For data on the total value and number of bitcoins in circulation, see https://blockchain.info. (Accessed on Mar. 31, 2014.)

[17] See Federal Reserve Statistical Release H.6 "Money Stock Measures" (Apr. 10, 2014) at http://www.federalreserve.gov/releases/h6/current/H6.pdf.

[18] https://www.coindesk.com. (Accessed on Apr.1, 2014.) This index is a composite price calculated as the simple average of bitcoin prices across leading global exchanges that meet certain criteria.

[19] https://blockchain.info. (Accessed on Apr. 1, 2014.)

[20] Federal Reserve. See http://www.federalreserve.gov/paymentsystems/fedach_yearlycomm.htm. (Accessed on Apr. 1, 2014.)

[21] https://coinmarketcap.com. (Accessed on Apr. 1, 2014.)

[22] https://coinmarketcap.com.(Accessed on Apr. 1, 2014.)

[23] Money laundering is the process of disguising or concealing the source of funds acquired illicitly to make the acquisition appear legitimate.

[24] Pub. L. No. 91-508, 84 Stat. 1114 (1970) (codified as amended at 12 U.S.C. §§ 1829(b), 1951-1959; 31 U.S.C. §§ 5311-5330); 31 C.F.R. chap. X. In 1994, the Secretary of the Treasury delegated overall authority for enforcement of, and compliance with, BSA and its implementing regulations related to money laundering to the Director of FinCEN. In the same year, the Secretary also delegated BSA examination authority to the prudential banking regulators. 31 C.F.R. § 1010.810(b)(1)-(5).

[25] FinCEN shares this responsibility with IRS, to which FinCEN has delegated examination authority for money services businesses. See 31 C.F.R. § 1010. 810(b)(8). IRS activities were outside the scope of our review. FinCEN has also delegated examination authority for BSA compliance to a number of other federal agencies, including the prudential banking regulators, CFTC, and SEC. See 31 C.F.R. § 1010.810(b). These agencies can also use their independent authorities to examine entities under their supervision for compliance with applicable BSA and anti-money-laundering requirements and regulations.

[26] Under 31 C.F.R. § 1010.100(ff)(1)-(7), money services businesses are generally defined as any of the following: (1) currency dealer or exchanger, (2) check casher, (3) issuer or seller of traveler's checks or money orders, (4) provider or seller of prepaid access, (5) money transmitter, and (6) the U.S. Postal Service. FinCEN's regulations define a money transmitter as a person that provides money transmission services, or any other person engaged in the transfer of funds. 31 C.F.R. § 1010.100(ff)(5)(i).The term money transmission services means the "acceptance of currency, funds, or other value that substitutes for currency to another location or person by any means." Id.

[27] FinCEN, *Application of FinCEN's Regulations to Persons Administering, Exchanging, or Using Virtual Currencies*, FIN-2013-G001, March 18, 2013. FinCEN defines an exchanger as a person engaged as a business in the exchange of virtual currency for real currency, funds, or other virtual currency. *Id.* FinCEN defines an administrator as a person engaged as a business in issuing (putting into circulation) a virtual currency, and who has the authority to redeem (to withdraw from circulation) such virtual currency. *Id.* An administrator or exchanger that (1) accepts and transmits a convertible virtual currency, or (2) buys or sells convertible virtual currency for any reason is a money transmitter under FinCEN's regulations.

[28] 31 C.F.R. § 1022.210, subpart C.

[29] 31 C.F.R. § 1020.220(a)(2)(i). Under the USA PATRIOT Act, financial institutions also must implement appropriate, specific, and, where necessary, enhanced, due diligence for correspondent accounts and private banking accounts established in the United States for non-U.S. persons. 31 U.S.C. § 5318(i).

[30] 31 U.S.C. § 5313(a); 31 C.F.R. § 1010.311.

[31] In addition, officials from the prudential banking regulators either stated or acknowledged that they would have authority to regulate a supervised entity that issued virtual currency, or cleared or settled transactions related to virtual currency.

[32] FinCEN, *Interagency Interpretive Guidance on Providing Banking Services to Money Services Businesses Operating in the United States*, April 26, 2005. FinCEN concurrently issued guidance to money services businesses that identified and explained the types of information and documentation that money services businesses were expected to have and provide to banking organizations. Bank holding companies are companies that own or control one or more banks. In the United States, most banks insured by FDIC are owned or controlled by a bank holding company.

[33] Under the risk-focused approach, those activities judged to pose the highest risk to an institution are to receive the most scrutiny by examiners.

[34] See 12 U.S.C. § 1786(q), § 1818(s) (federal banking agencies must promulgate regulations requiring insured depository institutions and credit unions to establish procedures regarding BSA compliance; regulators' examinations must include review of BSA compliance procedures); see also procedures for monitoring BSA compliance: 12 C.F.R. § 208.63 (Federal Reserve), 12 C.F.R. § 326.8 (FDIC), 12 C.F.R. § 748.2 (NCUA), and 12.C.F.R. § 21.21 (OCC).

[35] A civil money penalty is a punitive fine assessed for the violation of a law or regulation or for other misconduct. A cease-and-desist proceeding is a formal process that may result in an order that a party halt certain activities or practices; the order may also require the party to take affirmative action to correct the conditions resulting from the practices. See 12 U.S.C. § 1786(e), § 1818(b).

[36] Pub. L. No. 90-321, 92 Stat. 3728 (1978) (codified as amended at 15 U.S.C. §§ 1693-1693r). CFPB issues and enforces Regulation E, which implements the Electronic Fund Transfer Act (EFTA). EFTA establishes basic rights, liabilities, and responsibilities of consumers who use electronic fund transfer services and of financial institutions that offer these services.

[37] Pub. L. No. 111-203, § 1021(c)(5), 124 Stat. 1376, 1980 (2010) (codified at 12 U.S.C. § 5511(c)(5)). For example, section 1032(a) of the Dodd-Frank Act confers authority on CFPB "to prescribe rules to ensure that the features of any consumer financial product or service, both initially and over the term of the product or service, are fully, accurately, and effectively disclosed to consumers in a manner that permits consumers to understand the costs, benefits, and risks associated with the product or service, in light of the facts and circumstances." 12 U.S.C. § 5532(a). In prescribing such disclosure rules, section 1032 requires the Bureau to "consider available evidence about consumer awareness, understanding of, and responses to disclosures or communications about the risks, costs, and benefits of consumer financial products or services." 12 U.S.C. § 5532(c).

[38] Pub. L. No. 111-203, § 1013(b)(3), § 1021(c), 124 Stat. 1376, 1969, 1980 (2010) (codified at 12 U.S.C. §§ 5493(b)(3), 5511(c)).

[39] 15 U.S.C. §§ 80b-2(a)(11), 80b-11(g)-(h).

[40] See 15 U.S.C. § 80b-6(1)-(2); *SEC v. Capital Gains Research Bureau, Inc.*, et al., 375 U.S. 180 (1963).

[41] 17 C.F.R. § 240.15c3-1. SEC's net capital rule requires all broker-dealers to maintain a minimum level of net capital consisting of highly liquid assets. Assets that are not liquid are deducted in full when computing net capital.

[42] 7 U.S.C. § 2. Financial derivatives are financial instruments whose value is based on one or more underlying reference items. They are used to hedge risk or to exchange a floating rate of return for a fixed rate of return. In the virtual currency context, a derivative might be used to reduce exposure to volatility in virtual currency exchange rates.

[43] 7 U.S.C. §§ 1-26; 17 C.F.R. chap. I.

[44] The Commodity Exchange Act defines a commodity as certain agricultural goods and "all services, rights, and interests (except motion picture box office receipts, or any index, measure, value or data related to such receipts) in which contracts for future delivery are presently or in the future dealt in." 7 U.S.C. § 1a(9).

[45] Futures commission merchants are entities that solicit or accept orders for the purchase or sale of a commodity for future delivery on or subject to the rules of any exchange and that accept payment from or extend credit to those whose orders are accepted.

[46] One example would be a centralized virtual currency system that allowed users to make untraceable funds transfers.

[47] Pub. L. No. 91-508, 84 Stat. 1114 (codified as amended at 12 U.S.C. §§ 1829(b), 1951-1959; 31 U.S.C. §§ 5311-5330); Pub. L. No. 107-56, tit. III, 115 Stat. 272, 296-342 (International Money Laundering Abatement and Anti-Terrorist Financing Act of 2001) (codified at 31 U.S.C. §§ 5301-5318A) (to prevent, detect, and prosecute international money laundering); see also Money Laundering Suppression Act of 1994, Pub. L. No. 103-325, §§ 401-413, 108 Stat. 2160, 2243-2255 (codified at 31 U.S.C. § 5330 and scattered sections of U.S.C.) (requires money transmitting businesses to register with Treasury).

[48] 31 C.F.R. § 1020.410.

[49] Financial institutions are also required to obtain customer information to satisfy "know-your-customer" or "customer due diligence" identification programs as part of their anti-money laundering obligations, and financial institutions must subject certain bank accounts held by non-U.S. persons to enhanced due diligence procedures. See 31 U.S.C. § 5318(i).

[50] However, in a virtual currency transfer between individuals through a third-party intermediary (such as a virtual currency exchange), personally identifiable information is required to be collected if the transaction is for $3,000 or more. This requirement became effective in 2011. We discuss this requirement in the next section of this report.

[51] We discuss examples of such losses in the next section of this report.

[52] The next section of this report discusses an example of a fraud scheme involving a virtual-currency-based security.

[53] A chargeback is a payment reversal initiated by a consumer due, for example, to nondelivery of a purchased product.

[54] As previously noted, that privacy may be lost if a connection is established between a bitcoin address and its owner.

[55] Some industry observers have suggested that virtual currency system protocols may have applications beyond financial transactions. For example, just as the bitcoin protocol transfers and records ownership rights to currency, it could, in theory, be used to transfer and record ownership rights to stocks, among other things.

[56] *Bank Secrecy Act Regulations; Definitions and Other Regulations Relating to Money Services Businesses*, 76 Fed. Reg. 43585 (July 21, 2011).

[57] 31 C.F.R. § 1010.100(ff)(5)(i)(A).

[58] FinCEN, *Application of FinCEN's Regulations to Persons Administering, Exchanging, or Using Virtual Currencies*, FIN-2013-G001, March 18, 2013. This guidance addresses convertible virtual currency—that is, virtual currency which either has an equivalent value in real currency or acts as a substitute for real currency.

[59] According to FinCEN, virtual currency exchangers and administrators with U.S. customers must comply with BSA requirements, such as instituting anti-money-laundering controls, even if they are based outside of the United States.

[60] FinCEN's guidance defines a virtual currency user as "a person who obtains convertible virtual currency and uses it to purchase real or virtual goods or services on the user's own behalf." Although a user is not considered to be a money transmitter, FinCEN warns that a user's activities must still comply with other federal and state laws and regulations.

[61] Most states also regulate money services businesses and some have taken steps to address virtual currencies. For example, New York is developing licensing and regulatory requirements specific to virtual currency exchanges and Texas has issued a memorandum describing how current licensing requirements apply to virtual currency exchanges. FinCEN coordinates with its state counterparts to encourage application of FinCEN's guidance on virtual currencies as part of this process.

[62] FinCEN, *Application of FinCEN's Regulations to Virtual Currency Mining Operations*, FIN-2014-R001, January 30, 2014, and FinCEN, *Application of FinCEN's Regulations to Virtual Currency Software Development and Certain Investment Activity*, FIN-2014-R002, January 30, 2014.

[63] For example, a company that purchases and sells virtual currencies whenever such purchases and sales make investment sense according to the company's business plan is acting as a virtual currency user, not a virtual currency exchange.

[64] FinCEN, *Application of Money Services Business Regulations to the Rental of Computer Systems for Mining Virtual Currencies*, FIN-2014-R007, April 29, 2014.

[65] A Ponzi scheme is a type of investment fraud that involves the payment of purported returns to existing investors from funds contributed by new investors.

[66] *Securities and Exchange Commission v. Shavers*, No. 413-CV-416 (E.D. Texas Aug. 6, 2013).

[67] In addition, in March 2014, the Financial Industry Regulatory Authority, a self-regulatory organization for the securities industry, issued an investor alert about the risks of buying, using, and speculating in virtual currencies and the potential for related scams. See http://www.finra.org/Investors/ProtectYourself/InvestorAlerts/FraudsAndScams/P456458. Also, in April 2014, the North American Securities Administrators Association issued an investor advisory on virtual currencies, related investment risks, and the types of investments that might involve virtual currencies. See http://www.nasaa.org/30631/informed-investor-advisory-virtual-currency.

[68] http://www.investor.gov/news-alerts/investor-alerts/investor-alert-ponzi-schemes-using-virtual-currencies.

[69] http://www.investor.gov/news-alerts/investor-alerts/investor-alert-bitcoin-other-virtual-currency related-investments.

[70] Exchange-traded funds are commonly structured as open-end investment companies and offer investors a proportionate share in a pool of stocks, bonds, and other assets.

[71] Rule 506(c) is one of the exemptive rules under Regulation D that allow some businesses to offer and sell their securities without having to register the offer and sale of securities with SEC. Regulation D is designed to (1) simplify the previously existing rules and regulations, (2) eliminate any unnecessary restrictions that those rules and regulations place on small business issuers, and (3) achieve uniformity between state and federal exemptions to facilitate capital formation consistent with protecting investors.

[72] 17 C.F.R. § 230.506(c). Accredited investors include, among others, individuals whose net worth is more than $1 million (not including the value of their primary residence) or whose individual income exceeds at least $200,000 for the most recent 2 years (or joint income with a spouse exceeding $300,000 for those years) and a reasonable expectation of the same

income level in the current year. It also includes certain types of entities, such as insurance companies, banks, and corporations with assets exceeding $5 million. 17 C.F.R. § 230.501(a).

[73] As of March 31, 2014, these bitcoins were worth about $80 million, according to bitcoin prices from https://www.coindesk.com.

[74] 31 U.S.C. § 5318A. Section 311 of the USA PATRIOT Act grants the Secretary of the Treasury the authority, upon finding that reasonable grounds exist for concluding that a foreign jurisdiction, institution, class of transaction, or type of account is of "primary money laundering concern," to require domestic financial institutions and financial agencies to take certain "special measures" to address the primary money laundering concern.

[75] This case is being prosecuted jointly by the DOJ Criminal Division's Asset Forfeiture and Money Laundering Section and the U.S. Attorney's Office for the Southern District of New York.

[76] FFIEC is a formal interagency body empowered to prescribe uniform principles, standards, and report forms for the federal examination of financial institutions by the Federal Reserve, FDIC, NCUA, OCC, and CFPB, and to make recommendations to promote uniformity in the supervision of financial institutions.

[77] The Secret Service was mandated by the USA PATRIOT Act to establish a nationwide network of Electronic Crimes Task Forces. Pub. L. 107-56, § 105, 115 Stat 272, 277 (2001) (codified at 18 U.S.C. § 3056 note). The goal of the network is to bring together federal, state, and local law enforcement, as well as prosecutors, private industry, and academia to prevent, detect, and investigate various forms of electronic crime.

[78] The International Centre for Missing & Exploited Children is a nonprofit corporation that leads a movement to protect children from sexual exploitation and abduction. The Centre is involved in virtual currency issues because of connections between digital technologies that facilitate anonymity and commercial child pornography, sexual exploitation, and sex trafficking.

[79] Digital Economy Task Force, *The Digital Economy: Potential, Perils, and Promises* (March 2014).

[80] GAO, *Managing for Results: Key Considerations for Implementing Interagency Collaborative Mechanisms*, GAO-12-1022 (Washington, D.C.: Sept. 27, 2012).

[81] GAO, *Managing for Results: Implementation Approaches Used to Enhance Collaboration in Interagency Groups*, GAO-14-220 (Washington, D.C.: Feb. 14, 2014).

[82] CFPB (via the Office of Financial Education) is responsible for educating and empowering consumers to make better-informed financial decisions. Pub. L. No. 111-203, § 1013(d), 124 Stat. 1376, 1970 (2010).

[83] Congressional Research Service, *Bitcoin: Questions, Answers, and Analysis of Legal Issues* (Washington, D.C.: Dec. 20, 2013).

[84] Data from Coindesk.com. These bitcoins were worth approximately $390 million as of March 31, 2014. https://www.coindesk.com.

[85] For the Conference of State Bank Supervisors and the North American Securities Administrators Association joint model consumer guidance, see http://www.csbs.org/legislative/testimony/Documents/ModelConsumerGuidance--Virtual%20Currencies.pdf.

[86] These states include Alabama, California, Florida, Hawaii, Maryland, Massachusetts, Nevada, Washington, and Wisconsin.

[87] European Banking Authority, *Warning to Consumers on Virtual Currencies*, EBA/WRG/2013/01, Dec. 12, 2013. See http://www.eba.europa.eu/-/eba-warns-consumers-on-virtual-currencies.

[88] CFPB's complaint intake system is not specifically geared towards virtual currency complaints. However, in February 2014, CFPB ran a query of its Consumer Complaint Database to determine the number of complaints that had mentioned virtual currency or bitcoin and found that only 14 out of about 290,000 complaints met that condition.

In: Virtual Currencies
Editor: Kevin Lyndell
ISBN: 978-1-63463-129-7

Chapter 2

VIRTUAL ECONOMIES AND CURRENCIES: ADDITIONAL IRS GUIDANCE COULD REDUCE TAX COMPLIANCE RISKS*

United States Government Accountability Office

ABBRAVIATIONS

EBEI	Electronic Business and Emerging Issues
IRS	Internal Revenue Service
MMORPG	massively multiplayer online role-playing game

WHY GAO DID THIS STUDY

Recent years have seen the development of virtual economies, such as those within online role-playing games, through which individual participants can own and exchange virtual goods and services. Within some virtual economies, virtual currencies have been created as a medium of exchange for goods and services. Virtual property and currency can be exchanged for real goods, services, and currency, and virtual currencies have been developed

* This is an edited, reformatted and augmented version of The United States Government Accountability Office publication, GAO-13-516, Report to the Committee on Finance, U.S. Senate, dated May 2013.

outside of virtual economies as alternatives to government-issued currencies, such as dollars. These innovations raise questions about related tax requirements and potential challenges for IRS compliance efforts.

This report (1) describes the tax reporting requirements for virtual economies and currencies, (2) identifies the potential tax compliance risks of virtual economies and currencies, and (3) assesses how IRS has addressed the tax compliance risks of virtual economies and currencies.

To accomplish these objectives, GAO reviewed tax laws, IRS guidance and program documents, federal program internal control guidance, and interviewed IRS officials and knowledgeable experts on the topics.

What GAO Recommends

GAO recommends that IRS find relatively low-cost ways to provide information to taxpayers, such as on its website, on the basic tax reporting requirements for virtual currencies. In commenting on a draft of this report, IRS agreed with our recommendation.

What GAO Found

Transactions within virtual economies or using virtual currencies could produce taxable income in various ways, depending on the facts and circumstances of each transaction. For example, transactions within a "closed-flow" virtual currency system do not produce taxable income because a virtual currency can be used only to purchase virtual goods or services. An example of a closed-flow transaction is the purchase of items to use within an online game. In an "open-flow" system, a taxpayer who receives virtual currency as payment for real goods or services may have earned taxable income since the virtual currency can be exchanged for real goods or services or readily exchanged for government-issued currency, such as U.S. dollars.

Virtual economies and currencies pose various tax compliance risks, but the extent of actual tax noncompliance is unknown. Some identified risks include taxpayers not being aware that income earned through virtual economies or currencies is taxable or not knowing how to calculate such income.

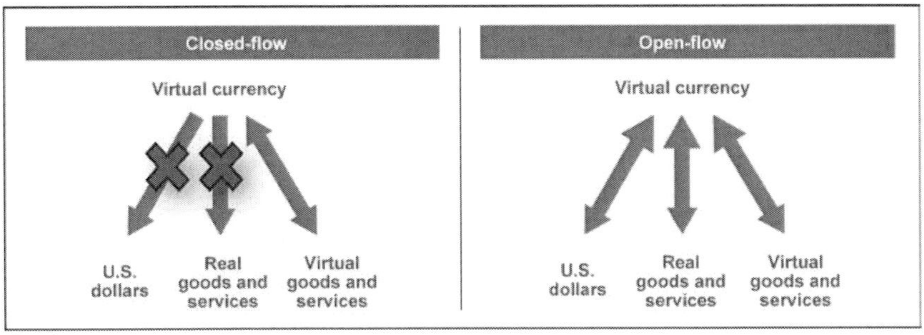

Source: GAO.

Because of the limited reliable data available on their size, it is difficult to determine how significant virtual economy and currency markets may be or how much tax revenue is at risk through their usage. Some experts with whom we spoke indicated a potential for growth in the use of virtual currencies.

Beginning in 2007, IRS assessed the tax compliance risks from virtual economies, and in 2009 posted information on its website on the tax consequences of virtual economy transactions. However, IRS has not provided taxpayers with information specific to virtual currencies because of other priorities, resource constraints, and the need to consider the use of these recently-developed currencies, according to IRS officials. By not issuing guidance, IRS may be missing an opportunity to address virtual currency tax compliance risks. Given the uncertain extent of noncompliance with virtual currency transactions, formal guidance, such as regulations, may not be warranted. According to IRS officials, formal guidance requires extensive review, which adds to development time and cost. However, IRS may be able to develop more timely and less costly informal guidance, which, according to IRS officials, requires less extensive review and can be based on other existing guidance. An example is the information IRS provides to taxpayers on its website on the tax consequences of virtual economy transactions. Posting such information would be consistent with IRS's strategy for preventing and minimizing taxpayers' noncompliance by helping them understand and meet their tax responsibilities.

***

May 15, 2013
The Honorable Max Baucus Chairman
The Honorable Orrin Hatch Ranking Member

Committee on Finance
United States Senate

Recent years have seen the development of virtual economies, such as those within online role-playing games, through which individual participants can earn and exchange virtual goods and services. Within some virtual economies, virtual currencies have been created as a medium of exchange for goods and services. Virtual property and currency can have economic value outside of virtual economies, such as when individuals trade these virtual goods for dollars or other government-issued currencies. More recently, virtual currencies have been developed outside of virtual economies as alternatives to government-issued currencies to exchange for real-world goods and services. These innovations raise questions about their related tax requirements and whether their increased adoption could pose challenges for the Internal Revenue Service (IRS) in its efforts to ensure tax compliance.

You asked us to review virtual economies and currencies and IRS's approach to addressing their tax implications. This report's objectives are to (1) describe the tax reporting requirements for virtual economies and currencies, (2) identify the potential tax compliance risks of virtual economies and currencies, and (3) assess how IRS has addressed the tax compliance risks of virtual economies and currencies.

To describe reporting requirements for virtual economies and currencies, we reviewed the Internal Revenue Code and applicable IRS regulations, including relevant sections of the Internal Revenue Manual, and interviewed IRS officials. We also reviewed academic articles and interviewed academics whose research focuses on virtual currencies and taxation of virtual transactions, as well as tax practitioners and representatives from the American Institute of Certified Public Accountants. We selected academics to interview based on criteria including the recognition and citations of their research in the relevant literature. We selected tax practitioners and representatives based on their association with an organization with widely-recognized expertise in federal tax matters.

To identify potential compliance risks associated with virtual currencies and virtual economies, we reviewed and analyzed legal and academic literature and government reports, including the National Taxpayer Advocate's 2008 Annual Report to Congress and the European Central Bank's October 2012 report on virtual currencies. We then discussed these compliance risks with knowledgeable experts, including the Bitcoin Foundation, a virtual currency user group; tax professionals, including members of the American Institute of

Certified Public Accountants; representatives from a company that publishes a virtual economy platform; and academics who have written about virtual currencies and taxation of virtual economy transactions. We selected experts based on criteria including their recognition and citations in the literature, and their expertise and recognition in representing taxpayers in federal tax matters or in representing virtual economy or currency concerns. We interviewed IRS officials knowledgeable on virtual economies and currencies and overall IRS tax compliance enforcement efforts. We also performed Internet searches to see what information was circulating for determining the proper tax treatment of virtual economy and currency transactions.

To assess how IRS has addressed compliance risks, we reviewed IRS documentation, including training manuals, examination guides, and internal reports detailing compliance challenges posed by virtual economies. We also interviewed knowledgeable IRS staff on the agency's efforts to learn about virtual economies and currencies and address them through compliance efforts. We compared IRS's efforts to federal program management guidance on gathering and monitoring information to identify and assess program risks, including the internal control standards for federal government and our *Internal Control Management and Evaluation Tool.*[1] Such guidance stipulates that agencies should have adequate mechanisms to identify risks to agency programs arising from external factors and that agencies should consider and, if appropriate, address the risks associated with technological advancements and developments and risks resulting from business and economic changes, among other types of changes. We also reviewed general IRS procedures and plans for providing information to taxpayers to help them comply with tax requirements included in IRS's Taxpayer Assistance Blueprint and related progress reports to Congress.[2]

BACKGROUND

We conducted this performance audit from September 2012 to May 2013 in accordance with generally accepted government auditing standards. Those standards require that we plan and perform the audit to obtain sufficient, appropriate evidence to provide a reasonable basis for our findings and conclusions based on our audit objectives. We believe that the evidence obtained provides a reasonable basis for our findings and conclusions based on our audit objectives.

There are no legal definitions for a virtual economy or currency, but generally, a virtual economy is comprised by the economic activities among a community of entities that interact within a virtual setting, such as an online, multi-user game. Virtual economies can be closed, meaning the economic activities and units of exchange used within the community do not interact with the real economy outside of the virtual environment setting, or they can be open, with some economic activity occurring in both the virtual setting and the real economy. A virtual currency is, generally, a digital unit of exchange that is not backed by a government-issued legal tender. Virtual currencies can be used entirely within a virtual economy, or can be used in lieu of a government-issued currency to purchase goods and services in the real economy. Some virtual economies may function similarly to barter exchanges,[3] where bartering is the exchange of goods or services in lieu of monetary payments. For example, a carpenter may build a desk for a dentist in exchange for dental work. Barter transactions are taxable transactions, and taxpayers must report the fair market value of the good or service received on their tax returns. Some of the variations in virtual currencies and their interaction with the real economy are shown in figure 1.

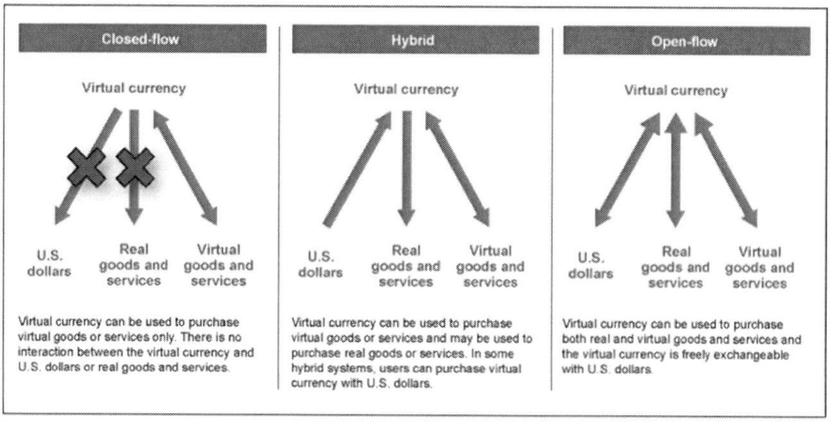

Source: GAO.

Figure 1. Types of Virtual Currency Systems.

In a "closed-flow" virtual currency system, a virtual currency can be used only within a game or virtual environment to purchase virtual goods or services, such as additional tools to use within a game. Virtual tools amassed by players can be traded in a game for other in-game assets or to advance to higher play levels, but they hold no value outside of the game and cannot be cashed out for dollars or other government-issued currencies.

In a hybrid system, one or more of the flows between the virtual currency and real dollars or goods and services is closed. For example, participants can purchase virtual currency with real dollars or earn virtual currency by completing tasks, such as taking surveys, and then use the currency to purchase real or virtual goods and services. However, the virtual currency might not be exchangeable back into real dollars. An example of a hybrid system is some massively multiplayer online role-playing games (MMORPG). MMORPGs allow users to create avatars, or graphical representations of themselves, that exist within a digital world and interact with other avatars around the globe to carry out tasks. Some MMORPGs operate as a closed-flow system, but some of these closed-flow systems can leak into the real economy via third-party transactions. Some MMORPGs, like World of Warcraft®, a large MMORPG, have third-party exchanges that allow users to exchange virtual goods for real dollars. This interaction between the virtual and real economies can be limited by the game's distributor through terms of use agreements.

In an "open-flow" system, virtual currencies can be used to purchase both real and virtual goods and services, as well as be readily exchanged for government-issued currency, such as U.S. dollars. One example of an open-flow currency designed primarily for use in a virtual economy is Second Life® Linden™ dollars. Second Life, a product of Linden Lab®, is a virtual economy created in 2003 that has its own virtual currency. "Residents" of Second Life create avatars and interact with other avatars in a user-defined and user-created environment. Within Second Life, residents can create virtual assets, such as buildings that they rent or sell to other residents, or operate virtual businesses, such as virtual clothing stores that sell virtual goods to other residents. Transactions taking place within Second Life use Linden Lab's virtual currency, Linden dollars. Second Life residents can sell their Linden dollars to other residents for U.S. dollars through the LindeX™ exchange, which uses third-party payment networks to process the payments and allows residents to cash out of the Second Life world.

An open-flow currency can also be developed and designed primarily to be used to purchase real goods and services outside an online game virtual economy. An example is bitcoin, a decentralized digital currency that uses a peer-to-peer computer network to move bitcoins around the world. Developed in 2009 by an anonymous programmer or programmers, bitcoin is a privately-issued digital currency that exists only as a long string of numbers and letters in a user's computer file. Bitcoins use cryptography to secure and safeguard against counterfeiting. Unlike U.S. dollars and other currencies, bitcoin is not government issued and does not have a physical coin or bill associated with its circulation, such as a Federal Reserve note. Bitcoin has grown in popularity since its introduction and, according to academics and user groups with whom we spoke, is the most widely circulated virtual currency available. Bitcoins act as a real world currency in that users pay for real goods and services, such as coffee or web development services, with bitcoins as opposed to U.S. dollars or other government-issued currencies. Third-party exchanges allow bitcoin users to exchange their bitcoins back to government-issued currencies, such as U.S. dollars, euro, or yen.

Bitcoins are created and entered into circulation through a process, called mining, that members of the bitcoin network perform. To perform the work of mining, bitcoin miners download free bitcoin software that they use to solve complex equations. These equations serve to verify the validity of bitcoin transactions by grouping several transactions into a block and mathematically proving that the transactions occurred and do not represent double spending of a bitcoin. When a miner's computer solves an equation, the bitcoin network accepts the block of transactions as valid and creates 25 new bitcoins and awards them to the successful miner.[4] By the bitcoin program's design, there will be a maximum of 21 million bitcoins in circulation once all bitcoins have been mined, which the program's design projects to be in the year 2140. In addition to mining new bitcoins, users can also acquire bitcoins already in circulation by purchasing them on third-party exchanges or accepting bitcoins as gifts or payments for goods or services. Figure 2 shows an example of how bitcoins enter circulation and how an individual can use bitcoins to pay for real goods or services.

Bitcoin transactions can be anonymous, since all that is needed to complete a transaction is a bitcoin address, which does not contain any personal identifying information. Only the private key holder knows the identity of the bitcoin address owner.

The size of the virtual economy and currency markets is unclear due to limitations in available data. For example, some companies that offer virtual economy platforms are private firms and do not report statistics about their virtual worlds' activities.

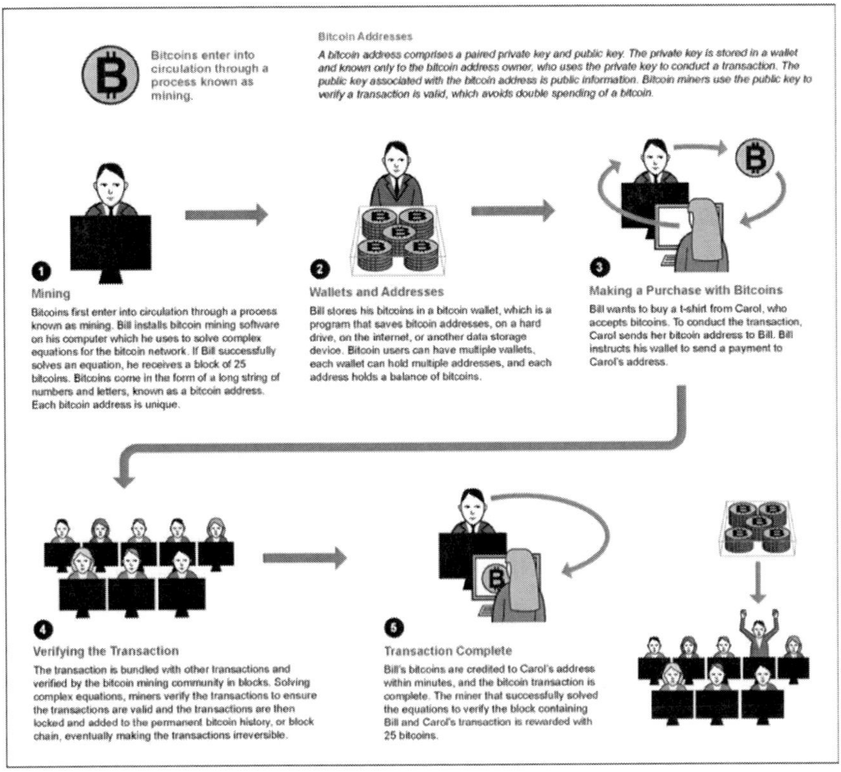

Source: GAO.

Figure 2. How Bitcoins Enter Circulation and Are Used in Transactions.

Further, due to the global nature of the Internet, borderless transactions, and an individual's ability to have multiple virtual economy or currency accounts, we did not find reliable data available indicating the use of virtual economies or currencies by individuals or exclusively by U.S. taxpayers.5 Even with these limitations, some data exist that may provide some context for the size of virtual economy and currency markets.

- According to bitcoin's peer-to-peer-network-generated statistics,6 as of May 1, 2013, approximately 11 million bitcoins were in circulation.7 Bitcoin exchange rates against the U.S. dollar historically have been volatile. From May 2012 through February 2013, prices ranged between $5 and $20 for 1 bitcoin. Prices increased through March 2013, and then from April 1, 2013, to May

1, 2013, ranged between $79 and over $237 for 1 bitcoin.8 In the same time period, the number of bitcoin transactions per day ranged from approximately 8,000 to 70,000 transactions per day.

- As of December 31, 2012, there were over 9.6 million active users of World of Warcraft, a large MMORPG, according to Blizzard Entertainment®, the company that develops and publishes the World of Warcraft games.
- According to Linden Lab, creators of Second Life, residents exchanged more than US$150 million worth of Linden dollars within Second Life's economy in the third quarter of 2010.

IRS is responsible for ensuring taxpayer compliance for all economic areas, including virtual economies and currencies. One mechanism that assists IRS in enforcing tax laws is information reporting, through which third parties report to IRS and taxpayers on certain taxpayer transactions. For example, subject to certain thresholds, third-party settlement organizations are required to report on Form 1099-K payments in settlement of third-party network transactions.[9] A common example of a third-party settlement organization is an online auction-payment facilitator, which operates as an intermediary between buyers and sellers by transferring funds between their accounts in settlement of purchases. Another type of third-party information reporting is performed by barter exchanges, which, generally, are organizations that facilitate barter transactions among exchange members. Such barter exchanges are required to report on Form 1099-B each member's barter transactions proceeds. Third-party information reporting is widely acknowledged to increase voluntary tax compliance, in part because taxpayers know that IRS is aware of their income.

Likewise, in its role in administering the tax code, IRS must implement the laws Congress enacts through detailed guidance. To accomplish this responsibility, IRS publishes several forms of guidance, such as regulations, revenue rulings and procedures, and notices. IRS also provides more informal guidance on its website based on factors such as perceived need, media coverage, or IRS staff identifying an emerging tax compliance issue. As outlined in IRS's Taxpayer Assistance Blueprint and related reports, a key part of IRS's strategy for preventing and minimizing noncompliance is to outreach to taxpayers to help them understand and meet their tax responsibilities. One of the guiding principles of this approach is to enhance IRS's website so that it becomes the first choice of taxpayers for obtaining the information they need to comply.

Virtual Economy and Currency Transactions May Be Taxable If They Produce Income

Transactions within virtual economies or using virtual currencies could produce taxable income in a number of ways depending on their specific facts and circumstances. U.S. tax laws and regulations generally require taxpayers to report and pay taxes on all income, regardless of the source from which the income was derived;[10] there are no additional rules specific to virtual currencies or economies. For example, similar to cash transactions, there are no third-party reporting requirements specific to virtual economy or currency transactions, as there are with some other types of electronic funds transactions, such as with transactions conducted through third-party payment networks. Taxpayers are required to account for any taxable income, including income that is not subject to third-party information reporting. The following examples show how some taxpayers may incur a tax liability when using a virtual currency for the three types of virtual currency systems described in the background of this report. We discussed these examples with IRS officials, who agreed with how we characterized the potential tax implications.

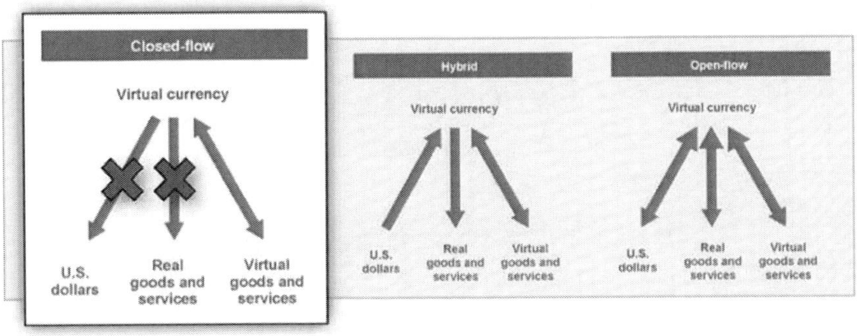

Source: GAO.

- David plays an online game through which he is issued money that he can use to purchase properties within the game. These properties have no value outside the game and David cannot exchange his online money for U.S. dollars. David has not engaged in a taxable transaction.

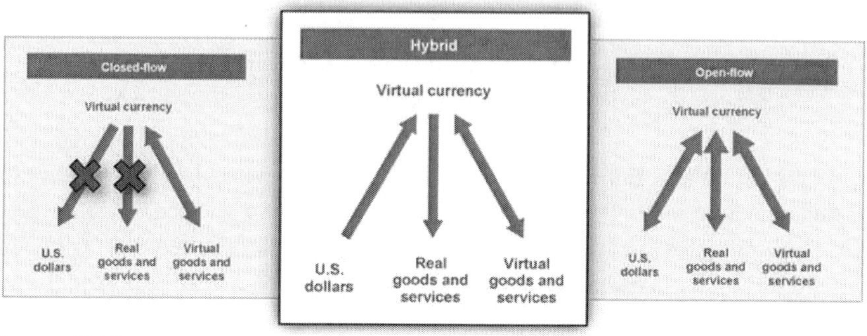

Source: GAO.

- Ann plays an online game and amasses virtual tools that are valuable to her avatar. The online game does not allow users to directly exchange their virtual tools for U.S. dollars, but rather they can do so using a third-party, making this a hybrid system. Ann uses a third-party exchange not affiliated with the online game to coordinate the transfer of her virtual tools to another player in exchange for U.S. dollars. The transfer is conducted by the third-party exchange and payment is mediated by a third-party payment network. Ann may have earned taxable income from the sale of these virtual tools.

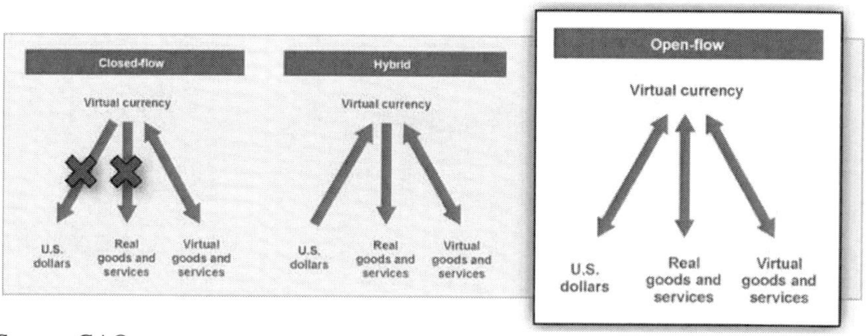

Source: GAO.

- John is a resident of Second Life. He rents virtual property to other residents who pay him in Linden dollars. At the end of the year, John exchanges his Linden dollars for U.S. dollars and realizes a profit. John may have earned taxable income from his activities in Second Life.

- Bill is a bitcoin miner. He successfully mines 25 bitcoins. Bill may have earned taxable income from his mining activities.
- Carol makes t-shirts and sells them over the Internet. She sells a t-shirt to Bill, who pays her with bitcoins. Carol may have earned taxable income from the sale of the t-shirt.

VIRTUAL ECONOMIES AND CURRENCIES POSE VARIOUS TAX COMPLIANCE RISKS, BUT THE EXTENT OF NONCOMPLIANCE IS UNKNOWN

IRS, tax experts, academics, and others have identified various tax compliance risks associated with virtual economies and currencies, including underreporting, mischaracterization, and evasion. These risks are not unique to virtual economies and currencies, as they also exist for other types of transactions, such as cash transactions, where there are not always clear records or third-party tracking and reporting of transactions. The tax compliance risks we identified for virtual economies and currencies are described below.

- *Taxpayer lack of knowledge of tax requirements.* Income is generally defined as any undeniable accessions to wealth, clearly realized, and over which the taxpayers have complete dominion.[11] The unsophisticated taxpayer may not properly identify income earned through virtual economies or currencies, such as virtual online game assets exchanged for real word currency, as taxable income. If taxpayers using virtual currencies turn to the Internet for tax help, they may find misinformation in the absence of clear guidance from IRS. For example, when we performed a simple Internet search for information on taxation of bitcoin transactions, we found a number of websites, wikis, and blogs that provided differing opinions on the tax treatment of bitcoins, including some that could lead taxpayers to believe that transacting in virtual currencies relieves them of their responsibilities to report and pay taxes.
- *Uncertainty over how to characterize income.* Even if taxpayers are aware that they may have a tax liability, they may be uncertain about the proper tax treatment of virtual transactions, according to tax experts, including academics and tax practitioners with whom we

spoke. For example, characterization depends on whether the virtual economy activity or virtual currency unit is to be treated as property, barter, foreign currency, or a financial instrument. According to some experts with whom we spoke, some virtual currency transactions could be considered barter transactions, which may not be an obvious characterization to unsophisticated taxpayers.[12] This characterization could result in noncompliance with requirements for reporting and paying tax on barter income.

- *Uncertainty over how to calculate basis for gains.* Income earned from virtual economy or currency transactions may not be taxable if it is equivalent to that from an occasional online garage sale, meaning occasional income from selling goods for less than their original purchase price. It may be difficult for individuals receiving income from virtual economies to determine their basis for calculating gains. For example, some online games require players to pay a monthly fee in exchange for use of the game and a monthly allowance of virtual currency. If a player then sells a virtual tool gained in the game for real money, calculating the basis for any taxable gain may be difficult for the unsophisticated taxpayer.
- *Challenges with third-party reporting.* Third-party information reporting requirements do not apply specifically to transactions using virtual economies or currencies. Virtual economy or currency transactions may be subject to third-party information reporting to the extent that these transactions involve the use of a third-party payment network to mediate the transaction and the taxpayer meets reporting threshold requirements.[13] Because virtual economy and currency transactions are inherently difficult to track, including identifying the true identities of the parties to the transaction, third-party information reporting may be difficult or prohibitively burdensome for some virtual economy and currency issuers to administer.
- *Evasion.* Some taxpayers may use virtual economies and currencies as a way to evade taxes. Because transactions can be difficult to trace and many virtual economies and currencies offer some level of anonymity, taxpayers may use them to hide taxable income.

Because of the limited reliable data available on their size, it is difficult to determine how significant virtual economy and currency markets may be or how much tax revenue is at risk through their usage. Some experts with whom we spoke indicated that there is potential for growth in the use of virtual currencies.

Additionally, the European Central Bank recently issued a report on virtual currencies, acknowledging their potential for future growth and interaction with the real economy.[14] If the use of virtual economies and currencies expands, it can be expected that associated revenue at risk of tax noncompliance will grow.

IRS HAS PROVIDED SOME GUIDANCE ON TAX REPORTING REQUIREMENTS FOR VIRTUAL ECONOMIES BUT NOT FOR VIRTUAL CURRENCIES USED OUTSIDE OF VIRTUAL ECONOMIES

IRS has assessed the tax compliance risks from virtual economies and virtual currencies used within those economies, and developed a plan to address them in a manner consistent with internal control standards. Beginning in 2007, IRS's Electronic Business and Emerging Issues (EBEI) policy group identified and surveyed internal and external information sources, gathered data on the industry, and collect trend information, among other efforts. EBEI determined that virtual economies presented opportunities for income underreporting and developed (1) a potential compliance strategy, including initiating a compliance improvement project to gather research data and analyze compliance trends, and (2) a potential action plan for specific compliance activities.

According to IRS compliance officials, IRS ultimately decided not to pursue these actions in light of available IRS resources and other higher priority needs. Also, IRS did not find strong evidence of the potential for tax noncompliance related to virtual economies, such as the number of U.S. taxpayers involved in such activity or the amount of federal tax revenue at risk.

However, in November 2009, based on EBEI having determined the need, IRS posted information on its website on the tax consequences of virtual economy transactions. The web page points out that, in general, taxpayers can receive income in the form of money, property, or services from a virtual economy, and that if taxpayers receive more income than they spend, they may be required to report their gains as taxable income.

The page further states that IRS has provided guidance on the tax treatment of issues similar to online gaming activities, including bartering, gambling, business, and hobby income, and provides links to IRS publications on those topics. IRS officials who were involved in issuing this guidance reported it cost less to make an online statement pointing taxpayers to existing guidance than it would have cost to develop and publish new guidance specific to virtual economies.

IRS has not assessed the tax compliance risks of open-flow virtual currencies developed and used outside of virtual economies. These types of currencies, generally, were introduced after IRS's last review of compliance related to virtual economy transactions. According to IRS compliance officials, IRS would learn about tax compliance issues related to virtual currencies as it would any other tax compliance issue, such as IRS examiners identifying compliance problems during examinations or taxpayers requesting guidance on how to comply with certain tax requirements. To date, these processes have not resulted in IRS identifying virtual currencies used outside of virtual economies as a compliance risk that warrants specific attention.

Likewise, IRS has not issued guidance specific to virtual currencies used outside of virtual economies due to competing priorities and resource constraints, and because the use of virtual currencies is a relatively recent development that requires further consideration before guidance can be issued, according to IRS's Office of Chief Counsel and compliance officials.[15] As previously discussed, taxpayers may be unaware that income from transactions using this type of virtual currency may be taxable, or if they are aware, uncertain on how to characterize it. By not issuing guidance, IRS may be missing an opportunity to address these compliance risks and minimize their impact and the potential for noncompliance. Given the uncertain extent of noncompliance related to virtual currency transactions, formal guidance, such as regulations, revenue rulings, or revenue notices, may not be warranted at this time.

According to officials from IRS's Office of Chief Counsel, these types of guidance require extensive review within IRS and the Department of the Treasury and, in some cases, public comment, which add to the time and cost of development. However, IRS may be able to develop informal guidance, which, according to Chief Counsel officials, requires less extensive agency review and can be based on other existing guidance. As such, IRS can develop informal guidance in a more timely and less costly manner than formal guidance, according to the officials.

An example of such informal guidance is the information IRS provides to taxpayers on its website on the tax consequences of virtual economy transactions. Posting such information to its website would be consistent with IRS's strategy for preventing and minimizing taxpayers' noncompliance by helping them understand and meet their tax responsibilities, as outlined in IRS's Taxpayer Assistance Blueprint.

CONCLUSION

Virtual economies and the use of virtual currencies intended as alternatives to government-issued currencies are a recent phenomenon, and the extent to which their use results in tax noncompliance is unknown. Given this uncertainty, available funding, and other priorities, IRS made a reasoned decision not to implement a compliance approach specific to virtual economies and currencies. However, IRS did see value in providing taxpayers with information on the tax consequences of virtual economy transactions, a low-cost step to potentially mitigate some of the noncompliance risk associated with such transactions. The uncertainty about the extent virtual currencies are used in taxable transactions and any associated tax noncompliance means that costly compliance activities are not merited at this time. However, the fact that misinformation is circulating and the possibility of growth in the use of virtual currencies outside virtual economies suggest that it would be prudent to take low-cost steps, if available, to mitigate potential compliance risks. The type of information IRS provided about virtual economy transactions is one model.

RECOMMENDATION FOR EXECUTIVE ACTION

To mitigate the risk of noncompliance from virtual currencies, the Commissioner of Internal Revenue should find relatively low-cost ways to provide information to taxpayers, such as the web statement IRS developed on virtual economies, on the basic tax reporting requirements for transactions using virtual currencies developed and used outside virtual economies.

AGENCY COMMENTS AND OUR EVALUATION

We sent a draft of this report to the Acting Commissioner of Internal Revenue for comment. In written comments, IRS agreed with our recommendation and stated it would provide information to taxpayers on the basic tax reporting requirements for transactions involving virtual currencies by linking to existing relevant guidance. IRS noted that it was aware of the tax compliance risks associated with virtual currencies and was taking other steps, such as developing training resources for agents, to address them. IRS also provided technical comments on our draft report, which we incorporated, as appropriate.

James R. White
Director, Tax Issues Strategic Issues

End Notes

[1] GAO, Internal Control Management and Evaluation Tool, GAO-01-1008G (Washington, D.C.: August 2001).

[2] The 2007 Taxpayer Assistance Blueprint—a 5-year strategic plan for improving service to taxpayers—is a collaborative effort of IRS, the National Taxpayer Advocate, and the IRS Oversight Board. Congress has received annual update reports on the implementation of the blueprint.

[3] The term "barter exchange" means any organization of members providing property or services who jointly contract to trade or barter such property or services. 26 U.S.C. § 6045.

[4] According to bitcoin's design, the number of bitcoins issued to successful miners will halve every time the network reaches 210,000 blocks, or approximately every four years. From inception through November 2012, rewards were 50 bitcoins. In 2016, rewards are expected to halve again to 12.5 bitcoins.

[5] Given these limitations, we did not test the reliability of data, such as the data generated from the bitcoin network, but are providing some figures to provide context for the possible size of these markets.

[6] http://blockchain.info. (Date accessed May 1, 2013.)

[7] Due to data limitations, it is difficult to calculate the velocity, or the rate at which bitcoins are spent, and the number of transactions between unique users in a given time period.

[8] https://mtgox.com. (Date accessed May 1, 2013.) https://mtgox.com operates the largest bitcoin exchange. The site has daily and monthly limits on how many bitcoins may be exchanged back to U.S. dollars or other virtual or government-issued currencies. These limits may be raised if users provide additional documentation confirming their identity.

[9] Third-party settlement organizations must file Form 1099-K if gross payments to a payee exceed $20,000 and there are more than 200 transactions with the payee in a given tax year.

[10] For federal tax purposes, all income is taxable, although the tax code excludes some items from income, such as gifts or inheritances, subject to exceptions, while it allows other items

to be deducted to reduce taxable income, subject to limitations and restrictions, such as trade or business expenses.

[11] Commissioner v. Glenshaw Glass Co., 348 U.S. 426 (1955).

[12] 26 U.S.C. § 6045 addresses barter exchanges and barter transactions.

[13] 26 U.S.C. § 6050W and applicable regulations define third-party payment networks.

[14] European Central Bank, Virtual Currency Schemes (Frankfurt am Main, Germany: October 2012).

[15] Although IRS has not issued guidance, another Department of the Treasury agency, the Financial Crimes Enforcement Network, recently issued interpretive guidance clarifying the treatment of persons creating, obtaining, distributing, exchanging, accepting, or transmitting virtual currencies. However, such guidance does not discuss the tax treatment of virtual currency transactions. FIN-2013-G001.

In: Virtual Currencies
Editor: Kevin Lyndell

ISBN: 978-1-63463-129-7

Chapter 3

APPLICATION OF FINCEN'S REGULATIONS TO PERSONS ADMINISTERING, EXCHANGING, OR USING VIRTUAL CURRENCIES*

Financial Crimes Enforcement Network

GUIDANCE

FIN-2013-G001
Issued: March 18, 2013
Subject: Application of FinCEN's Regulations to Persons Administering, Exchanging, or Using Virtual Currencies

The Financial Crimes Enforcement Network ("FinCEN") is issuing this interpretive guidance to clarify the applicability of the regulations implementing the Bank Secrecy Act ("BSA") to persons creating, obtaining, distributing, exchanging, accepting, or transmitting virtual currencies.[1] Such persons are referred to in this guidance as "users," "administrators," and "exchangers," all as defined below.[2] A user of virtual currency is ***not*** an MSB under FinCEN's regulations and therefore is not subject to MSB registration,

* This is an edited, reformatted and augmented version of Guidance Document, FIN-2013-G001, issued by the U.S. Department of the Treasury, Financial Crimes Enforcement Network, March 18, 2013.

reporting, and recordkeeping regulations. However, an administrator or exchanger ***is*** an MSB under FinCEN's regulations, specifically, a money transmitter, unless a limitation to or exemption from the definition applies to the person. An administrator or exchanger is not a provider or seller of prepaid access, or a dealer in foreign exchange, under FinCEN's regulations.

Currency vs. Virtual Currency

FinCEN's regulations define currency (also referred to as "real" currency) as "the coin and paper money of the United States or of any other country that [i] is designated as legal tender and that [ii] circulates and [iii] is customarily used and accepted as a medium of exchange in the country of issuance."[3] In contrast to real currency, "virtual" currency is a medium of exchange that operates like a currency in some environments, but does not have all the attributes of real currency. In particular, virtual currency does not have legal tender status in any jurisdiction. This guidance addresses "convertible" virtual currency. This type of virtual currency either has an equivalent value in real currency, or acts as a substitute for real currency.

Background

On July 21, 2011, FinCEN published a Final Rule amending definitions and other regulations relating to money services businesses ("MSBs").[4] Among other things, the MSB Rule amends the definitions of dealers in foreign exchange (formerly referred to as "currency dealers and exchangers") and money transmitters. On July 29, 2011, FinCEN published a Final Rule on Definitions and Other Regulations Relating to Prepaid Access (the "Prepaid Access Rule").[5] This guidance explains the regulatory treatment under these definitions of persons engaged in virtual currency transactions.

Definitions of User, Exchanger, and Administrator

This guidance refers to the participants in generic virtual currency arrangements, using the terms "user," "exchanger," and "administrator."[6] A *user* is a person that obtains virtual currency to purchase goods or services.[7] An *exchanger* is a person engaged as a business in the exchange of virtual currency for real currency, funds, or other virtual currency. An *administrator* is a person engaged as a business in issuing (putting into circulation) a virtual currency, and who has the authority to redeem (to withdraw from circulation) such virtual currency.

USERS OF VIRTUAL CURRENCY

A user who obtains convertible virtual currency and uses it to purchase real or virtual goods or services is ***not*** an MSB under FinCEN's regulations.[8] Such activity, in and of itself, does not fit within the definition of "money transmission services" and therefore is not subject to FinCEN's registration, reporting, and recordkeeping regulations for MSBs.[9]

ADMINISTRATORS AND EXCHANGERS OF VIRTUAL CURRENCY

An administrator or exchanger that (1) accepts and transmits a convertible virtual currency or (2) buys or sells convertible virtual currency for any reason ***is*** a money transmitter under FinCEN's regulations, unless a limitation to or exemption from the definition applies to the person.[10] FinCEN's regulations define the term "money transmitter" as a person that provides money transmission services, or any other person engaged in the transfer of funds. The term "money transmission services" means "the acceptance of currency, funds, or other value that substitutes for currency from one person *and* the transmission of currency, funds, or other value that substitutes for currency to another location or person by any means."[11]

The definition of a money transmitter does not differentiate between real currencies and convertible virtual currencies. Accepting and transmitting anything of value that substitutes for currency makes a person a money transmitter under the regulations implementing the BSA.[12] FinCEN has reviewed different activities involving virtual currency and has made determinations regarding the appropriate regulatory treatment of administrators and exchangers under three scenarios: brokers and dealers of e-currencies and e-precious metals; centralized convertible virtual currencies; and de-centralized convertible virtual currencies.

a. E-Currencies and E-Precious Metals

The first type of activity involves electronic trading in e-currencies or e-precious metals.[13] In 2008, FinCEN issued guidance stating that as long as a broker or dealer in real currency or other commodities accepts and transmits funds solely for the purpose of effecting a *bona fide* purchase or sale of the real currency or other commodities for or with a customer, such person is not acting as a money transmitter under the regulations.[14]

However, if the broker or dealer transfers funds between a customer and a third party that is not part of the currency or commodity transaction, such transmission of funds is no longer a fundamental element of the actual transaction necessary to execute the contract for the purchase or sale of the currency or the other commodity. This scenario is, therefore, money transmission.[15] Examples include, in part, (1) the transfer of funds between a customer and a third party by permitting a third party to fund a customer's account; (2) the transfer of value from a customer's currency or commodity position to the account of another customer; or (3) the closing out of a customer's currency or commodity position, with a transfer of proceeds to a third party. Since the definition of a money transmitter does not differentiate between real currencies and convertible virtual currencies, the same rules apply to brokers and dealers of e-currency and e-precious metals.

b. Centralized Virtual Currencies

The second type of activity involves a convertible virtual currency that has a centralized repository. The administrator of that repository will be a money transmitter to the extent that it allows transfers of value between persons or from one location to another. This conclusion applies, whether the value is denominated in a real currency or a convertible virtual currency. In addition, any exchanger that uses its access to the convertible virtual currency services provided by the administrator to accept and transmit the convertible virtual currency on behalf of others, including transfers intended to pay a third party for virtual goods and services, is also a money transmitter.

FinCEN understands that the exchanger's activities may take one of two forms. The first form involves an exchanger (acting as a "seller" of the convertible virtual currency) that accepts real currency or its equivalent from a user (the "purchaser") and transmits the value of that real currency to fund the user's convertible virtual currency account with the administrator. Under FinCEN's regulations, sending "value that substitutes for currency" to another person or to another location constitutes money transmission, unless a limitation to or exemption from the definition applies.[16] This circumstance constitutes transmission *to another location*, namely from the user's account at one location (e.g., a user's real currency account at a bank) to the user's convertible virtual currency account with the administrator. It might be argued that the exchanger is entitled to the exemption from the definition of "money transmitter" for persons involved in the sale of goods or the provision of services. Under such an argument, one might assert that the exchanger is merely providing the service of connecting the user to the administrator and that the transmission of value is integral to this service. However, this exemption does not apply when the only services being provided are money transmission services.[17]

The second form involves a *de facto* sale of convertible virtual currency that is not completely transparent. The exchanger accepts currency or its equivalent from a user and privately credits the user with an appropriate portion of the exchanger's own convertible virtual currency held with the administrator of the repository. The exchanger then transmits that internally credited value to third parties at the user's direction. This constitutes transmission *to another person*, namely each third party to which transmissions are made at the user's direction. To the extent that the convertible virtual currency is generally understood as a substitute for real currencies, transmitting the convertible virtual currency at the direction and for the benefit of the user constitutes money transmission on the part of the exchanger.

c. De-Centralized Virtual Currencies

A final type of convertible virtual currency activity involves a de-centralized convertible virtual currency (1) that has no central repository and no single administrator, and (2) that persons may obtain by their own computing or manufacturing effort.

A person that creates units of this convertible virtual currency and uses it to purchase real or virtual goods and services is a user of the convertible virtual currency and not subject to regulation as a money transmitter. By contrast, a person that creates units of convertible virtual currency and sells those units to another person for real currency or its equivalent is engaged in transmission to another location and is a money transmitter. In addition, a person is an exchanger and a money transmitter if the person accepts such de-centralized convertible virtual currency from one person and transmits it to another person as part of the acceptance and transfer of currency, funds, or other value that substitutes for currency.

PROVIDERS AND SELLERS OF PREPAID ACCESS

A person's acceptance and/or transmission of convertible virtual currency cannot be characterized as providing or selling prepaid access because prepaid access is limited to real currencies.[18]

DEALERS IN FOREIGN EXCHANGE

A person must exchange the currency of two or more countries to be considered a dealer in foreign exchange.[19] Virtual currency does not meet the criteria to be considered "currency" under the BSA, because it is not legal tender. Therefore, a person who accepts real currency in exchange for virtual currency, or *vice versa*, is not a dealer in foreign exchange under FinCEN's regulations.

* * * * *

Financial institutions with questions about this guidance or other matters related to compliance with the implementing regulations of the BSA may contact FinCEN's Regulatory Helpline at (800) 949-2732.

End Notes

[1] FinCEN is issuing this guidance under its authority to administer the Bank Secrecy Act. See Treasury Order 180-01 (March 24, 2003). This guidance explains only how FinCEN

characterizes certain activities involving virtual currencies under the Bank Secrecy Act and FinCEN regulations. It should not be interpreted as a statement by FinCEN about the extent to which those activities comport with other federal or state statutes, rules, regulations, or orders.

[2] FinCEN's regulations define "person" as "an individual, a corporation, a partnership, a trust or estate, a joint stock company, an association, a syndicate, joint venture, or other unincorporated organization or group, an Indian Tribe (as that term is defined in the Indian Gaming Regulatory Act), and all entities cognizable as legal personalities." 31 CFR § 1010.100(mm).

[3] 31 CFR § 1010.100(m).

[4] Bank Secrecy Act Regulations – Definitions and Other Regulations Relating to Money Services Businesses, 76 FR 43585 (July 21, 2011) (the "MSB Rule"). This defines an MSB as "a person wherever located doing business, whether or not on a regular basis or as an organized or licensed business concern, wholly or in substantial part within the United States, in one or more of the capacities listed in paragraphs (ff)(1) through (ff)(7) of this section. This includes but is not limited to maintenance of any agent, agency, branch, or office within the United States." 31 CFR § 1010.100(ff).

[5] Final Rule – Definitions and Other Regulations Relating to Prepaid Access, 76 FR 45403 (July 29, 2011),

[6] These terms are used for the exclusive purpose of this regulatory guidance. Depending on the type and combination of a person's activities, one person may be acting in more than one of these capacities.

[7] How a person engages in "obtaining" a virtual currency may be described using any number of other terms, such as "earning," "harvesting," "mining," "creating," "auto-generating," "manufacturing," or "purchasing," depending on the details of the specific virtual currency model involved. For purposes of this guidance, the label applied to a particular process of obtaining a virtual currency is not material to the legal characterization under the BSA of the process or of the person engaging in the process.

[8] As noted above, this should not be interpreted as a statement about the extent to which the user's activities comport with other federal or state statutes, rules, regulations, or orders. For example, the activity may still be subject to abuse in the form of trade-based money laundering or terrorist financing. The activity may follow the same patterns of behavior observed in the "real" economy with respect to the purchase of "real" goods and services, such as systematic over- or under-invoicing or inflated transaction fees or commissions.

[9] 31 CFR § 1010.100(ff)(1-7).

[10] FinCEN's regulations provide that whether a person is a money transmitter is a matter of facts and circumstances. The regulations identify six circumstances under which a person is not a money transmitter, despite accepting and transmitting currency, funds, or value that substitutes for currency. 31 CFR § 1010.100(ff)(5)(ii)(A)–(F).

[11] 31 CFR § 1010.100(ff)(5)(i)(A).

[12] Ibid.

[13] Typically, this involves the broker or dealer electronically distributing digital certificates of ownership of real currencies or precious metals, with the digital certificate being the virtual currency. However, the same conclusions would apply in the case of the broker or dealer issuing paper ownership certificates or manifesting customer ownership or control of real currencies or commodities in an account statement or any other form. These conclusions would also apply in the case of a broker or dealer in commodities other than real currencies or precious metals. A broker or dealer of e-currencies or e-precious metals that engages in

money transmission could be either an administrator or exchanger depending on its business model.

[14] Application of the Definition of Money Transmitter to Brokers and Dealers in Currency and other Commodities, FIN-2008-G008, Sept. 10, 2008. The guidance also notes that the definition of money transmitter excludes any person, such as a futures commission merchant, that is "registered with, and regulated or examined by...the Commodity Futures Trading Commission."

[15] In 2011, FinCEN amended the definition of money transmitter. The 2008 guidance, however, was primarily concerned with the core elements of the definition – accepting and transmitting currency or value – and the exemption for acceptance and transmission integral to another transaction not involving money transmission. The 2011 amendments have not materially changed these aspects of the definition.

[16] See footnote 11 and adjacent text.

[17] 31 CFR § 1010.100(ff)(5)(ii)(F).

[18] This is true even if the person holds the value accepted for a period of time before transmitting some or all of that value at the direction of the person from whom the value was originally accepted. FinCEN's regulations define "prepaid access" as "access to funds or the value of funds that have been paid in advance and can be retrieved or transferred at some point in the future through an electronic device or vehicle, such as a card, code, electronic serial number, mobile identification number, or personal identification number." 31 CFR § 1010.100(ww). Thus, "prepaid access" under FinCEN's regulations is limited to "access to funds or the value of funds." If FinCEN had intended prepaid access to cover funds denominated in a virtual currency or something else that substitutes for real currency, it would have used language in the definition of prepaid access like that in the definition of money transmission, which expressly includes the acceptance and transmission of "other value that substitutes for currency." 31 CFR § 1010.100(ff)(5)(i) .

[19] FinCEN defines a "dealer in foreign exchange" as a "person that accepts the currency, or other monetary instruments, funds, or other instruments denominated in the currency, of one or more countries in exchange for the currency, or other monetary instruments, funds, or other instruments denominated in the currency, of one or more other countries in an amount greater than $1,000 for any other person on any day in one or more transactions, whether or not for same-day delivery." 31 CFR § 1010.100(ff)(1).

In: Virtual Currencies
Editor: Kevin Lyndell

ISBN: 978-1-63463-129-7

Chapter 4

APPLICATION OF FINCEN'S REGULATIONS TO VIRTUAL CURRENCY MINING OPERATIONS*

Financial Crimes Enforcement Network

FIN-2014-R001
Issued: January 30, 2014
Subject: Application of FinCEN's Regulations to Virtual Currency Mining Operations

Dear [ ]:

This responds to your letter of June 1, 2013, seeking an administrative ruling from the Financial Crimes Enforcement Network ("FinCEN") on behalf of [the Company], about [the Company]'s possible status as a money services business ("MSB") under the Bank Secrecy Act ("BSA"). Specifically, you ask whether certain ways of disposing of the Bitcoins mined by [the Company] would make [the Company] a money transmitter under the BSA.

You state that [the Company] mines Bitcoins. You further state that the Bitcoins that [the Company] has mined have not yet been used or transferred, but that [the Company] may decide to use this virtual currency to purchase

* This is an edited, reformatted and augmented version of regulatory document, FIN-2014-R001, issued by the U.S. Department of the Treasury, Financial Crimes Enforcement Network, January 30, 2014.

goods or services, convert the virtual currency into currency of legal tender and use the currency to purchase goods and services, or transfer the virtual currency to the owner of the company. You ask in your letter whether any of these transactions would make [the Company] a money transmitter under the BSA.

On July 21, 2011, FinCEN published a Final Rule amending definitions and other regulations relating to MSBs (the "Rule").[1] The amended regulations define an MSB as "a person wherever located doing business, whether or not on a regular basis or as an organized business concern, wholly or in substantial part within the United States, in one or more of the capacities listed in paragraphs (ff)(1) through (ff)(6) of this section. This includes but is not limited to maintenance of any agent, agency, branch, or office within the United States."[2]

BSA regulations, as amended, define the term "money transmitter" to include a person that provides money transmission services, or any other person engaged in the transfer of funds. The term "money transmission services" means the acceptance of currency, funds, or other value that substitutes for currency from one person *and* the transmission of currency, funds, or other value that substitutes for currency to another location or person by any means.[3] The regulations also stipulate that whether a person is a money transmitter is a matter of facts and circumstances, and identifies circumstances under which a person's activities would not make such person a money transmitter.[4]

On March 18, 2013, FinCEN issued guidance on the application of FinCEN's regulations to transactions in virtual currencies (the "guidance").[5] FinCEN's regulations define currency (also referred to as "real" currency) as "the coin and paper money of the United States or of any other country that [i] is designated as legal tender and that [ii] circulates and [iii] is customarily used and accepted as a medium of exchange in the country of issuance."[6] In contrast to real currency, "virtual" currency is a medium of exchange that operates like a currency in some environments, but does not have all the attributes of real currency. In particular, virtual currency does not have legal tender status in any jurisdiction. The guidance addresses "convertible" virtual currency. This type of virtual currency either has an equivalent value in real currency, or acts as a substitute for real currency.

For purposes of the guidance, FinCEN refers to the participants in generic virtual currency arrangements, using the terms "exchanger," "administrator," and "user." An *exchanger* is a person engaged as a business in the exchange of virtual currency for real currency, funds, or other virtual currency. An *administrator* is a person engaged as a business in issuing (putting into circulation) a virtual currency, and who has the authority to redeem (to withdraw from circulation) such virtual currency. A *user* is a person that obtains virtual currency to purchase goods or services on the user's own behalf.

The guidance makes clear that an administrator or exchanger of convertible virtual currencies that (1) accepts and transmits a convertible virtual currency or (2) buys or sells convertible virtual currency in exchange for currency of legal tender or another convertible virtual currency for any reason (including when intermediating between a user and a seller of goods or services the user is purchasing on the user's behalf) is a money transmitter under FinCEN's regulations, unless a limitation to or exemption from the definition applies to the person.[7] The guidance also makes clear that "a user who obtains convertible virtual currency and uses it to purchase real or virtual goods or services is *not* an MSB under FinCEN's regulations." FinCEN understands your letter to amount to a request to elaborate on this last statement in the specific context of a user that obtains the convertible virtual currency Bitcoin by mining.

How a user obtains a virtual currency may be described using any number of other terms, such as "earning," "harvesting," "mining," "creating," "auto-generating," "manufacturing," or "purchasing," depending on the details of the specific virtual currency model involved. The label applied to a particular process of obtaining a virtual currency is not material to the legal characterization under the BSA of the process or of the person engaging in the process to send that virtual currency or its equivalent value to any other person or place. What is material to the conclusion that a person is not an MSB is not the mechanism by which a person obtains the convertible virtual currency, but what the person uses the convertible virtual currency for, and for whose benefit.

FinCEN understands that Bitcoin mining imposes no obligations on a Bitcoin user to send mined Bitcoin to any other person or place for the benefit of another. Instead, the user is free to use the mined virtual currency or its equivalent for the user's own purposes, such as to purchase real or virtual goods and services for the user's own use. To the extent that a user mines Bitcoin and uses the Bitcoin solely for the user's own purposes and not for the benefit of another, the user is *not* an MSB under FinCEN's regulations, because these activities involve neither "acceptance" nor "transmission" of the convertible virtual currency and are not the transmission of funds within the meaning of the Rule. This is the case whether the user mining and using the Bitcoin is an individual or a corporation, and whether the user is purchasing goods or services for the user's own use, paying debts previously incurred in the ordinary course of business, or (in the case of a corporate user) making distributions to shareholders. Activities that, in and of themselves, do not constitute accepting and transmitting currency, funds or the value of funds, are activities that do not fit within the definition of "money transmission services" and therefore are not subject to FinCEN's registration, reporting, and recordkeeping regulations for MSBs.[8]

From time to time, as your letter has indicated, it may be necessary for a user to convert Bitcoin that it has mined into a real currency or another convertible virtual currency, either because the seller of the goods or services the user wishes to purchase will not accept Bitcoin, or because the user wishes to diversify currency holdings in anticipation of future needs or for the user's own investment purposes. In undertaking such a conversion transaction, the user is not acting as an exchanger, notwithstanding the fact that the user is accepting a real currency or another convertible virtual currency and transmitting Bitcoin, so long as the user is undertaking the transaction solely for the user's own purposes and not as a business service performed for the benefit of another. A user's conversion of Bitcoin into a real currency or another convertible virtual currency, therefore, does not in and of itself make the user a money transmitter.[9]

FinCEN therefore concludes that, under the facts you have provided, [the Company] would be a user of Bitcoin, and not an MSB, to the extent that it uses Bitcoin it has mined: (a) to pay for the purchase of goods or services, pay debts it has previously incurred (including debts to its owner(s)), or make distributions to owners; or (b) to purchase real currency or another convertible virtual currency, so long as the real currency or other convertible virtual currency is used solely in order to make payments (as set forth above) or for [the Company]'s own investment purposes. Any transfers to third parties at the behest of sellers, creditors, owners, or counterparties involved in these transactions should be closely scrutinized, as they may constitute money transmission. (See footnotes 8 and 9 above.) And of course, should [the Company] engage in any other activity constituting acceptance and transmission of either currency of legal tender or virtual currency, it may be engaged in money transmission activities that would be subject to the requirements of the BSA.

This ruling is provided in accordance with the procedures set forth at 31 CFR Part1010 Subpart G. In arriving at the conclusions in this administrative ruling, we have relied upon the accuracy and completeness of the representations you made in your communications with us. Nothing precludes FinCEN from arriving at a different conclusion or from taking other action should circumstances change or should any of the information you have provided prove inaccurate or incomplete. We reserve the right, after redacting your name and address, and similar identifying information for your clients, to publish this letter as guidance to financial institutions in accordance with our regulations.[10] You have fourteen days from the date of this letter to identify any other information you believe should be redacted and the legal basis for redaction.

If you have questions about this ruling, please contact FinCEN's regulatory helpline at (703) 905-3591.

Sincerely, //signed//

Jamal El-Hindi Associate Director Policy Division

End Notes

[1] Bank Secrecy Act Regulations – Definitions and Other Regulations Relating to Money Services Businesses, 76 FR 43585 (July 21, 2011).

[2] 31 CFR § 1010.100(ff).

[3] 31 CFR § 1010.100(ff)(5)(i)(A) and (B).

[4] 31 CFR § 1010.100(ff)(5)(ii).

[5] FIN-2013-G001, "Application of FinCEN's Regulations to Persons Administering, Exchanging, or Using Virtual Currencies," March 18, 2013.

[6] 31 CFR § 1010.100(m).

[7] The definition of "money transmitter" in FinCEN's regulations defines six sets of circumstances – variously referred to as limitations or exemptions – under which a person is not a money transmitter, despite accepting and transmitting currency, funds, or value that substitutes for currency. 31 CFR § 1010.100(ff)(5)(ii)(A)-(F).

[8] However, a user wishing to purchase goods or services with Bitcoin it has mined, which pays the Bitcoin to a third party at the direction of a seller or creditor, may be engaged in money transmission. A number of older FinCEN administrative rulings, although not directly on point because they interpret an older version of the regulatory definition of MSBs, discuss situations involving persons that would have been exempted from MSB status, but for their payments to third parties not involved in the original transaction. See FIN-2008-R004 (Whether a Foreign Exchange Consultant is a Currency Dealer or Exchanger or Money Transmitter - 05/09/2008); FIN-2008-R003 (Whether a Person That is Engaged in the Business of Foreign Exchange Risk Management is a Currency Dealer or Exchanger or Money Transmitter - 05/09/2008); FIN-2008-R002 (Whether a Foreign Exchange Dealer is a Currency Dealer or Exchanger or Money Transmitter - 05/09/2008).

[9] As noted in footnote 8 above, however, a user engaging in such a transaction, which pays the Bitcoin to a third party at the direction of the counterparty, may be engaged in money transmission.

[10] 31 CFR §§ 1010.711-717.

In: Virtual Currencies
Editor: Kevin Lyndell

ISBN: 978-1-63463-129-7

Chapter 5

APPLICATION OF FINCEN'S REGULATIONS TO VIRTUAL CURRENCY SOFTWARE DEVELOPMENT AND CERTAIN INVESTMENT ACTIVITY*

Financial Crimes Enforcement Network

FIN-2014-R002
Issued: January 30, 2014
Subject: Application of FinCEN's Regulations to Virtual Currency Software Development and Certain Investment Activity

Dear [ ]:

This responds to your letters of May 21, 2013 and July 10, 2013, seeking an administrative ruling from the Financial Crimes Enforcement Network ("FinCEN") regarding the status of [ ] (the "Company") as a money services business ("MSB") under the Bank Secrecy Act ("BSA"). Specifically, you ask whether the periodic investment of the Company in convertible virtual currency, and the production and distribution of software to facilitate the

* This is an edited, reformatted and augmented version of regulatory document, FIN-2014-R002, issued by the U.S. Department of the Treasury, Financial Crimes Enforcement Network, January 30, 2014.

Company's purchase of virtual currency for purposes of its own investment, would make the Company a money transmitter under the BSA.

In your May 21, 2013 letter, you state that the Company intends to produce a piece of software that will facilitate the Company's purchase of virtual currency from sellers, by automating the collection of the virtual currency and the payment of the equivalent in currency of legal tender. The seller would initiate the process via the software's interface, offering its virtual currency to the Company, choosing among several options for a means of receiving the equivalent in currency of legal tender (check, credit to a designated credit, debit, or prepaid card, or payment processed through a third-party money transmitter), and paying a transaction fee. The software would not be sold or provided to any third party for resale, and it would be reserved for the sole use of the Company's counterparties.

Your addendum of July 10, 2013 clarifies that the Company intends to limit its activities to investing in convertible virtual currencies for its own account, purchasing virtual currency from sellers and reselling the currency at the Company's discretion, whenever such purchases and sales make investment sense according to the Company's business plan. The seller would offer its virtual currency to the Company via the software discussed above, and the Company would sell all or part of its virtual currency at a virtual currency exchange after receipt from the seller, at a time of the Company's choosing based on the Company's own investment decisions.

BSA Obligations of the Company as a Software Provider

On July 21, 2011, FinCEN published a Final Rule amending definitions and other regulations relating to MSBs (the "Rule").[1] The amended regulations define an MSB as "a person wherever located doing business, whether or not on a regular basis or as an organized business concern, wholly or in substantial part within the United States, in one or more of the capacities listed in paragraphs (ff)(1) through (ff)(6) of this section. This includes but is not limited to maintenance of any agent, agency, branch, or office within the United States."[2]

BSA regulations, as amended, define the term "money transmitter" to include a person that provides money transmission services, or any other person engaged in the transfer of funds. The term "money transmission services" means the acceptance of currency, funds, or other value that substitutes for currency from one person *and* the transmission of currency, funds, or other value that substitutes for currency to another location or person by any means.[3] The regulations also stipulate that whether a person is a money transmitter is a matter of facts and circumstances, and identifies circumstances under which a person's activities would not make such person a money transmitter.[4]

The production and distribution of software, in and of itself, does not constitute acceptance and transmission of value, even if the purpose of the software is to facilitate the sale of virtual currency. As a result, the Company's production and distribution of its contemplated software would not make the Company a money transmitter subject to BSA regulation.[5]

BSA Obligations of the Company as an Investor in Virtual Currencies

On March 18, 2013, FinCEN issued guidance on the application of FinCEN's regulations to transactions in virtual currencies (the "guidance").[6] FinCEN's regulations define currency (also referred to as "real" currency) as "the coin and paper money of the United States or of any other country that [i] is designated as legal tender and that [ii] circulates and [iii] is customarily used and accepted as a medium of exchange in the country of issuance."[7] In contrast to real currency, "virtual" currency is a medium of exchange that operates like a currency in some environments, but does not have all the attributes of real currency. In particular, virtual currency does not have legal tender status in any jurisdiction.

The guidance addresses "convertible" virtual currency. This type of virtual currency either has an equivalent value in real currency, or acts as a substitute for real currency.

For purposes of the guidance, FinCEN refers to the participants in generic virtual currency arrangements, using the terms "exchanger," "administrator," and "user." An *exchanger* is a person engaged as a business in the exchange of virtual currency for real currency, funds, or other virtual currency. An *administrator* is a person engaged as a business in issuing (putting into circulation) a virtual currency, and who has the authority to redeem (to withdraw from circulation) such virtual currency. A *user* is a person that obtains virtual currency to purchase goods or services on the user's own behalf.

The guidance makes clear that an administrator or exchanger of convertible virtual currencies that (1) accepts and transmits a convertible virtual currency or (2) buys or sells convertible virtual currency in exchange for currency of legal tender or another convertible virtual currency for any reason (including when intermediating between a user and a seller of goods or services the user is purchasing on the user's behalf) is a money transmitter under FinCEN's regulations, unless a limitation to or exemption from the definition applies to the person.[8] The guidance also makes clear that "a user who obtains convertible virtual currency and uses it to purchase real or virtual goods or services is *not* an MSB under FinCEN's regulations."

How a user engages in obtaining a virtual currency may be described using any number of other terms, such as "earning," "harvesting," "mining," "creating," "auto-generating," "manufacturing," or "purchasing," depending on the details of the specific virtual currency model involved. The label applied to a particular process of obtaining a virtual currency is not material to the legal characterization under the BSA of the process or of the person engaging in the process to send that virtual currency or its equivalent value to any other person or place. What is material to the conclusion that a person is not an MSB is not the mechanism by which person obtains the convertible virtual currency, but what the person uses the convertible virtual currency for, and for whose benefit. Activities that, in and of themselves, do not constitute accepting and transmitting currency, funds or the value of funds do not fit within the definition of "money transmission services" and therefore are not subject to FinCEN's registration, reporting, and recordkeeping regulations for MSBs.[9]

To the extent that the Company purchases and sells convertible virtual currency, paying and receiving the equivalent value in currency of legal tender to and from counterparties, all exclusively as investments for its own account, it is not engaged in the business of exchanging convertible virtual currency for currency of legal tender for other persons. In effect, when the Company invests in a convertible virtual currency for its own account, and when it realizes the value of its investment, it is acting as a user of that convertible virtual currency within the meaning of the guidance. As a result, to the extent that the Company limits its activities strictly to investing in virtual currency for its own account, it is not acting as a money transmitter and is not an MSB under FinCEN's regulations. However, any transfers to third parties at the behest of the Company's counterparties, creditors, or owners entitled to direct payments should be closely scrutinized, as they may constitute money transmission. (See footnote 10 to this ruling.)

If the Company were to provide services to others (including investment-related or brokerage services) that involved the accepting and transmitting of convertible virtual currency, or the exchange of convertible virtual currency for currency of legal tender or another convertible virtual currency, of course, additional analysis would be necessary to determine the Company's regulatory status and obligations with respect to such activity.[10] In addition, should the Company begin to engage as a business in the exchange of virtual currency against currency of legal tender (or even against other convertible virtual currency), the Company would become a money transmitter under FinCEN's regulations. Under such circumstances, the Company would have to register with FinCEN, implement an effective, risk-based anti-money laundering program, and comply with the recordkeeping, reporting, and transaction monitoring requirements applicable to money transmitters.

This ruling is provided in accordance with the procedures set forth at 31 CFR Part1010 Subpart G.[11] In arriving at the conclusions in this administrative ruling, we have relied upon the accuracy and completeness of the representations you made in your communications with us. Nothing precludes FinCEN from arriving at a different conclusion or from taking other action should circumstances change or should any of the information you have provided prove inaccurate or incomplete. We reserve the right, after redacting your name and address, and similar identifying information for your clients, to publish this letter as guidance to financial institutions in accordance with our regulations.[12] You have fourteen days from the date of this letter to identify any other information you believe should be redacted and the legal basis for redaction.

If you have questions about this ruling, please contact FinCEN's regulatory helpline at (703) 905-3591.

Sincerely, //signed//

Jamal El-Hindi Associate Director Policy Division

End Notes

[1] Bank Secrecy Act Regulations – Definitions and Other Regulations Relating to Money Services Businesses, 76 FR 43585 (July 21, 2011).

[2] 31 CFR § 1010.100(ff).

[3] 31 CFR § 1010.100(ff)(5)(i)(A) and (B).

[4] 31 CFR § 1010.100(ff)(5)(ii).

[5] A number of older FinCEN administrative rulings, although not directly on point because they interpret an older version of the regulatory definition of MSBs, explain the application of our definitions in comparable situations. See, e.g., FIN-2009-R001, "Whether Certain Operations of a Service Provider to Prepaid Stored Value Program Participants is a Money Services Business," January 22, 2009, available at http://www.fincen.gov/statutes_regs/guidance/pdf/fin-2009-r001.pdf.

[6] FIN-2013-G001, "Application of FinCEN's Regulations to Persons Administering, Exchanging, or Using Virtual Currencies," March 18, 2013.

[7] 31 CFR § 1010.100(m).

[8] The definition of "money transmitter" in FinCEN's regulations defines six sets of circumstances – variously referred to as limitations or exemptions – under which a person is not a money transmitter, despite accepting and transmitting currency, funds, or value that substitute for currency. 31 CFR § 1010.100(ff)(5)(ii)(A)-(F).

[9] However, a user wishing to purchase goods or services with a convertible virtual currency it has obtained, which pays the convertible virtual currency to a third party at the direction of a seller or creditor, may be engaged in money transmission. A number of older FinCEN administrative rulings, although not directly on point because they interpret an older version of the regulatory definition of MSBs, discuss situations involving persons that would have been exempted from MSB status, but for their payments to third parties not involved in the original transaction. See FIN-2008-R004 (Whether a Foreign Exchange Consultant is a Currency Dealer or Exchanger or Money Transmitter - 05/09/2008); FIN-2008-R003 (Whether a Person That is Engaged in the Business of Foreign Exchange Risk Management is a Currency Dealer or Exchanger or Money Transmitter - 05/09/2008); FIN-2008-R002 (Whether a Foreign Exchange Dealer is a Currency Dealer or Exchanger or Money Transmitter - 05/09/2008).

[10] For example, providing specific brokerage-related services might require the Company to be registered with the Securities and Exchange Commission (SEC) or the Commodities and Futures Trading Commission (CFTC), in which case the Company would be covered under the BSA as a securities broker-dealer or a commodities or futures trader. If the Company did not fall under SEC or CFTC supervision, then the extent to which its money transmission activities were integral to the non-money transmission services it provided would need to be considered in order to determine whether the Company could claim an exemption from the money transmitter definition under 31 CFR § 1010.100(ff)(5)(ii)(F), or would qualify as a money transmitter under FinCEN's regulations.

[11] Your subsequent e-mail communication of September 24, 2013 has informed us that you received a subpoena from the New York State Department of Financial Services on August 9, 2013 regarding the Company's activities. Although you have not informed us, and we have not by other means become aware, of the substance of any investigation to which this subpoena may relate, we have waived the requirement in our regulations that you certify that the question at issue in this administrative ruling is not applicable to any ongoing investigation. See 31 CFR §§ 1010.711(a)(4).

[12] 31 CFR §§ 1010.711-717.

In: Virtual Currencies
Editor: Kevin Lyndell
ISBN: 978-1-63463-129-7

Chapter 6

APPLICATION OF MONEY SERVICES BUSINESS REGULATIONS TO THE RENTAL OF COMPUTER SYSTEMS FOR MINING VIRTUAL CURRENCY*

Financial Crimes Enforcement Network

FIN-2014-R007
Issued: April 29, 2014
Subject: Application of Money Services Business regulations to the rental of computer systems for mining virtual currency

Dear [ ]:

This responds to your letter mailed to us on February 26, 2014, seeking an administrative ruling from the Financial Crimes Enforcement Network ("FinCEN") regarding the status of [ ] (the "Company") as a money services business ("MSB") under the Bank Secrecy Act ("BSA"). Specifically, you ask whether the rental of computer systems for mining virtual currency would make the Company an administrator of virtual currency or a money transmitter under the BSA. Based on the following analysis of the facts and circumstances

* This is an edited, reformatted and augmented version of regulatory document, FIN-2014-R007, issued by the U.S. Department of the Treasury, Financial Crimes Enforcement Network, April 29, 2014.

described in your letter, FinCEN finds that the Company is not functioning as an administrator of virtual currency and that the Company's renting of mining computer systems to third parties does not make the Company a money transmitter under BSA regulations.

You state that the Company has developed a computer system that mines crypto currencies. At times, the company rents this system to third parties in exchange for a payment based on the rental period, which may extend from 24 hours to 30 days. The third party will furnish the Company with limited information about its mining pool, which the Company will enter into the system so the third party benefits directly and exclusively from the mining work. All virtual currency mined by the third party remains the third party's property, and the Company has no access to the third party wallet, nor receives or pays virtual currency on the third party's behalf.

On July 21, 2011, FinCEN published a Final Rule amending definitions and other regulations relating to MSBs (the "Rule").[1] The amended regulations define an MSB as "a person wherever located doing business, whether or not on a regular basis or as an organized business concern, wholly or in substantial part within the United States, in one or more of the capacities listed in paragraphs (ff)(1) through (ff)(6) of this section. This includes but is not limited to maintenance of any agent, agency, branch, or office within the United States."[2]

BSA regulations, as amended, define the term "money transmitter" to include a person that provides money transmission services, or any other person engaged in the transfer of funds. The term "money transmission services" means the acceptance of currency, funds, or other value that substitutes for currency from one person *and* the transmission of currency, funds, or other value that substitutes for currency to another location or person by any means.[3]

On March 18, 2013, FinCEN issued guidance on the application of FinCEN's regulations to transactions in virtual currencies (the "guidance").[4] FinCEN's regulations define currency (also referred to as "real" currency) as "the coin and paper money of the United States or of any other country that [i] is designated as legal tender and that [ii] circulates and [iii] is customarily used and accepted as a medium of exchange in the country of issuance."[5] In contrast to real currency, "virtual" currency is a medium of exchange that operates like a currency in some environments, but does not have all the attributes of real currency. In particular, virtual currency does not have legal tender status in any jurisdiction. The guidance addresses "convertible" virtual currency. This type of virtual currency either has an equivalent value in real currency, or acts as a substitute for real currency.

For purposes of the guidance, FinCEN refers to the participants in generic virtual currency arrangements, using the terms "user," "exchanger," and "administrator." A *user* is a person that obtains virtual currency to purchase goods or services on the user's own behalf. FinCEN has determined that users are not money transmitters. An *exchanger* is a person engaged as a business in the exchange of virtual currency for real currency, funds, or other virtual currency. An *administrator* is a person engaged as a business in issuing (putting into circulation) a virtual currency, and who has the authority to redeem (to withdraw from circulation) such virtual currency. Both exchangers and administrators may operate as money transmitters depending on the specific facts and circumstances. According to your letter, the Company does not engage in the activities of an exchanger or administrator. Instead, the Company provides a rental service to those interested in using your computer system for mining virtual currencies administered by other entities. As such, FinCEN finds that the Company is not functioning as an administrator of virtual currency.

Further, FinCEN regulations stipulate that whether a person is a money transmitter is a matter of facts and circumstances, and identifies circumstances under which a person's activities would not make such person a money transmitter. The rental of computer systems to third parties is not an activity covered by FinCEN regulations. The regulations specifically exempt from money transmitter status a person that only provides the delivery, communication, or network data access services used by a money transmitter to supply money transmission services.[6] Based on this exemption, and on the description of the service offered by the Company, we find that, even if the Company rents a computer system to third parties that will use it to obtain convertible virtual not make the Company a money transmitter subject to BSA regulation.[7]

This ruling is provided in accordance with the procedures set forth at 31 CFR Part 1010 Subpart G. In arriving at the conclusions in this administrative ruling, we have relied upon the accuracy and completeness of the representations you made in your communications with us. Nothing precludes FinCEN from arriving at a different conclusion or from taking other action should circumstances change or should any of the information you have provided prove inaccurate or incomplete. We reserve the right, after redacting your name and address, and similar identifying information for your clients, to publish this letter as guidance to financial institutions in accordance with our regulations.[8] You have fourteen days from the date of this letter to identify any other information you believe should be redacted and the legal basis for redaction.

If you have questions about this ruling, please contact FinCEN's regulatory helpline at (703) 905-3591.

Sincerely, //signed//

Jamal El-Hindi Associate Director Policy Division

End Notes

[1] Bank Secrecy Act Regulations – Definitions and Other Regulations Relating to Money Services Businesses, 76 FR 43585 (July 21, 2011).

[2] 31 CFR § 1010.100(ff).

[3] 31 CFR § 1010.100(ff)(5)(i)(A) and (B).

[4] FIN-2013-G001, "Application of FinCEN's Regulations to Persons Administering, Exchanging, or Using Virtual Currencies," March 18, 2013.

[5] 31 CFR § 1010.100(m).

[6] 31 CFR § 1010.100(ff)(5)(ii)(A).

[7] A number of older FinCEN administrative rulings, although not directly on point because they interpret an older version of the regulatory definition of MSBs, explain the application of our definitions in comparable situations. See, e.g., FIN-2009-R001, "Whether Certain Operations of a Service Provider to Prepaid Stored Value Program Participants is a Money Services Business," January 22, 2009, available at http://www.fincen.gov/statutes_regs/guidance/pdf/fin-2009-r001.pdf.

[8] 31 CFR §§ 1010.711-717.

In: Virtual Currencies
Editor: Kevin Lyndell

ISBN: 978-1-63463-129-7

Chapter 7

BITCOIN: QUESTIONS, ANSWERS, AND ANALYSIS OF LEGAL ISSUES*

Craig K. Elwell, M. Maureen Murphy and Michael V. Seitzinger

SUMMARY

Bitcoin first appeared in January 2009, the creation of a computer programmer using the pseudonym Satoshi Nakamoto. His invention is an open source (its controlling computer code is open to public view), peer to peer (transactions do not require a third-party intermediary such as PayPal or Visa), digital currency (being electronic with no physical manifestation). The Bitcoin system is private, but with no traditional financial institutions involved in transactions. Unlike earlier digital currencies that had some central controlling person or entity, the Bitcoin network is *completely decentralized*, with all parts of transactions performed by the users of the system.

With a Bitcoin transaction there is no third party intermediary. The buyer and seller interact directly (peer to peer) but their identities are encrypted and no personal information is transferred from one to the other. However, unlike a fully anonymous transaction, there is a transaction record. A full transaction record of every Bitcoin and every Bitcoin user's encrypted identity is maintained on the public ledger. For

* This is an edited, reformatted and augmented version of a Congressional Research Service publication R43339, prepared for Members and Committees of Congress, dated July 15, 2014.

this reason Bitcoin transactions are thought to be pseudonymous, not anonymous. Although the scale of Bitcoin use has increased substantially, it still remains small in comparison to traditional electronic payments systems such as credit cards and the use of dollars as a circulating currency.

Congress is interested in Bitcoin because of concerns about its use in illegal money transfers, concerns about its effect on the ability of the Federal Reserve to meet its objectives (of stable prices, maximum employment, and financial stability), and concerns about the protection of consumers and investors who might use it.

Bitcoin offers users the advantages of lower transaction costs, increased privacy, and long term protection of loss of purchasing power from inflation. However, there are also a number of disadvantages that could hinder wider use. These include sizable volatility of the price of Bitcoins, uncertain security from theft and fraud, and a long term deflationary bias that encourages the hoarding of Bitcoins.

Bitcoin also raises a number of legal and regulatory concerns including its potential for facilitating money laundering, its treatment under federal securities law, and its status in the regulation of foreign exchange trading.

The digital currency called Bitcoin has been in existence since 2009 and for most of that time it remained little more than a technological curiosity of interest to a small segment of the population. However, over the last year and a half, Bitcoin use has grown substantially; attention by the press has surged, and recently Bitcoin caught the attention of Congress, being the subject of two Senate hearings.[1]

This report has three major sections. The first section answers some basic questions about Bitcoin and the operation of the Bitcoin network and its interaction with the current dollar-based monetary system. The second section summarizes likely reasons for and against widespread Bitcoin adoption. The third section discusses legal and regulatory matters that have been raised by Bitcoin and other digital currencies.

SOME BASIC QUESTIONS

What Is Bitcoin? [1]

Bitcoin first appeared in January 2009, the creation of a computer programmer using the pseudonym Satoshi Nakamoto. His invention is an open source (its controlling computer code is open to public view), peer to peer (transactions do not require a third-party intermediary such as PayPal or Visa), digital currency (being electronic with no physical manifestation).[2]

Like the U.S. dollar, the Bitcoin is a *fiat currency* in that it is not redeemable for some amount of another commodity, such as an ounce of gold. Unlike the dollar, a Bitcoin is not legal tender nor is it backed by any government or any other legal entity, nor is its supply determined by a central bank. The Bitcoin system is private, but with no traditional financial institutions involved in transactions. Unlike earlier digital currencies that had some central controlling person or entity, the Bitcoin network is *completely decentralized*, with all parts of transactions performed by the users of the system.

How Does the Bitcoin System Work?

Bitcoin is sometimes referred to as a *cryptocurrency* because it relies on the principles of cryptography (communication that is secure from view of third parties) to validate transactions and govern the production of the currency itself. Each Bitcoin and each user is encrypted with a unique identity and each transaction is recorded on a decentralized public ledger (also called a *blockchain*) that is visible to all computers on the network, but does not reveal any personal information about the involved parties. The public ledger verifies that the buyer has the amount of Bitcoin being spent and has transferred that amount to the account of the seller.

The public ledger is a unique attribute of Bitcoin (and other cryptocurrencies) because it solves the so called *double spending* problem (i.e., spending money you do not own by use of forgery or counterfeiting) and the need for a trusted third party (such as a bank or credit card company) to verify the integrity of electronic transactions between a buyer and a seller.

How Are Bitcoins Obtained?

To interact on the Bitcoin network users first need to download the free and open-source software. Once connected to the network, there are three ways to obtain Bitcoins. First, a user can exchange conventional money (e.g., dollars, yen, and euros) for a fee on an online exchange (e.g., Okcoin,

Coinbase, and Kraken). The exchange fee falls with the size of the transaction, ranging from 0.5% for small transactions down to 0.2% for large transactions.

The price of Bitcoin relative to other currencies is determined by supply and demand. In mid-July 2014, a single Bitcoin was valued at around $600. However, the price has been quite volatile, having been above $1,100 in December 2013, and below $400 in mid-April 2014.[3]

Second, a user can obtain Bitcoins in exchange for the sale of goods or services, as when a merchant accepts Bitcoin from a buyer for the sale of his product.

Third, a user can generate Bitcoins through a process called *mining.* Mining involves applying the user's computer's processing power to solve a complex math problem to discover new Bitcoins. The probability of an individual discovering Bitcoins through mining is proportional to the amount of computer processing power that can be applied. This prospect is likely to be very small for the typical office or home computer. The difficulty of the math problem is such that Bitcoins will be discovered at a limited and predictable rate system wide.

Therefore, the supply of Bitcoins does not depend on the monetary policy of a virtual central bank. In this regard, although a fiat currency, the Bitcoin system's operation is similar to the growth of money under a gold standard, although historically the amount of gold mined was more erratic than the growth of the supply of Bitcoins is purported to be. Depending on one's perspective this attribute can be a virtue or a vice.

Currently, about 13 million Bitcoins are in circulation. However, the total number of Bitcoins that can be generated is arbitrarily capped at 21 million coins, which is predicted to be reached in 2140. Also, because a Bitcoin is divisible to *eight* decimal places, the maximum amount of spendable units is more than 2 *quadrillion* (i.e., 2000 trillion).

Purchased or mined Bitcoins are thereafter stored in a digital wallet on the user's computer or at an online wallet service.

Are Bitcoin Transactions Anonymous?

Bitcoin transactions are not truly anonymous.[4] An example of an anonymous transaction is an exchange for cash between two strangers. In this case, no personal information need be revealed nor does there need to be a record of the transaction. At the other extreme a non-anonymous transaction is a typical online purchase using a credit card. This transaction requires validation by a third-party intermediary to whom the buyer's and seller's identities and pertinent financial information is known and who maintains a record of the transaction. A Bitcoin transaction falls between these two extremes.

With a Bitcoin transaction there is no third-party intermediary. The buyer and seller interact directly (peer to peer), but their identities are encrypted and no personal information is transferred from one to the other. However, unlike a fully anonymous transaction, there is a transaction record. A full transaction record of every Bitcoin and every Bitcoin user's encrypted identity is maintained on the public ledger. For this reason Bitcoin transactions are thought to be pseudonymous, not anonymous.

Because of the public ledger, researchers have found that, using sophisticated computer analysis, transactions involving large quantities of Bitcoin can be tracked and claim that if paired with current law enforcement tools it would be possible to gain a lot of information on the persons moving the Bitcoins.[5] Also, if Bitcoin exchanges (where large transactions are most likely to occur) are to be fully compliant with the bank secrecy regulations (i.e., anti-money laundering laws) required of other financial intermediaries, Bitcoin exchanges will be required to collect personal data on their customers, limiting further the system's ability to maintain the user's pseudonymity.

What Is the Scale of Bitcoin Use?

Despite significant growth since its inception, Bitcoins scale of use remains that of a "niche" currency. In mid-July 2014, the total number of Bitcoins in circulation globally is about 13 million, up about 1 million coins from a year earlier. With its recent market price of near $600, Bitcoin's current market capitalization (price x number of coins in circulation) exceeds $8 billion. However, large swings in the price of Bitcoin have caused that market capitalization to exhibit similarly large changes during the year. As recently as December 2013, with Bitcoin exchanging at near $1,100, the market capitalization was above $140 billion. During 2014, Bitcoin daily transaction volume fluctuated in a range of between $40 million and $50 million, representing between 40,000 to 80,000 daily transactions.[6]

For comparison, in June 2014 the U.S. money supply (the sum of currency, demand deposits, saving deposits including money market saving accounts) was about $11.3 trillion (about 1,000 times larger.)[7] The credit card company Visa reports that for 2013 its total dollar volume was $6.9 trillion, with an average number of daily individual transactions of near 24 million.[8] In 2013, *daily* transactions in dollars on global foreign exchange markets averaged over $4 trillion.[9]

Would Bitcoins Affect the Fed's Conduct of Monetary Policy?

The Federal Reserve conducts monetary policy to affect the flow of money and credit to the economy in order to achieve stable prices, maximum employment, and financial market stability. At Bitcoin's current scale of use, it is likely too small to significantly affect the Fed's ability to conduct monetary policy and achieve those three goals. However, if the scale of use were to grow substantially larger, there could be reason for some concern. *Conceptually*, Bitcoin could have an impact on the conduct of monetary policy to the extent that it would (1) substantially affect the quantity of money or (2) influence the velocity (rate of circulation) of money through the economy by reducing the demand for dollars.

Regarding the money supply, if Bitcoin transactions occur on a *pre-paid* basis whereby Bitcoins enter into circulation when dollars are exchanged and then are withdrawn from circulation when exchanged back to dollars, the net effect on the money supply would be small.

Regarding the velocity of money, if the increase in the use of Bitcoin leads to a decrease in need for holding dollars, it would increase the dollar's velocity of circulation and tend to increase the money supply associated with any given amount of base money (currency in circulation plus bank reserves held with the Fed). In this case, for the Fed to maintain the same degree of monetary accommodation, it would need to undertake a compensating tightening of monetary policy. At a minimum, a substantial use of Bitcoins could make the measurement of velocity more uncertain, and judging the appropriate stance of monetary policy uncertain.

Also, a substantial decrease in the use of dollars would also tend to reduce the size of the Fed's balance sheet and introduce another factor into its consideration of how to affect short-term interest rates (the instrument for implementing monetary policy). However, the Fed's ability to conduct monetary policy rests on its ability to increase or decrease the reserves of the banking system through open market operations. So long as there is a sizable demand by banks for liquid dollar-denominated reserves, the Fed would likely continue to be able to influence interest rates and conduct monetary policy.[10] [11]

Again, any sizable effect on the U.S. monetary system is predicated on Bitcoin's scale of use becoming substantially greater than it is at present. An important force that is likely to hinder such growth in Bitcoin use is the strong preference for dollar use generated by what economists call *network externalities* (i.e., the value of a product or service is dependent on the number of others using it). Network externalities create a self-generating demand for a dominant currency. The more often a currency is used as a medium of exchange, the more liquid it becomes and the lower are the costs of transacting in it, leading, in turn, to its becoming even more attractive to new users. Network externalities create a tendency toward having one dominant currency and confer a substantial *incumbency advantage* to the dollar in both domestic and international use. The legal tender status of the dollar, discussed below, reinforces this advantage. [12]

The U.S. economy reaps considerable benefit from having a single well-defined and stable monetary unit to work as a medium of exchange and unit of account to facilitate its vast number of daily economic transactions. If greater use of Bitcoin (and other cryptocurrencies) leads to multiple monetary units, these benefits could be threatened, particularly if these new currencies continue to exhibit a high degree of price volatility. (Price volatility is discussed more fully below.)

REASONS FOR AND AGAINST WIDER USE OF BITCOIN

Why Would One Want to Use Bitcoins?

Bitcoin purportedly offers three potential benefits to users: lower transaction costs, increased privacy, and no erosion of purchasing power due to inflation.

Lower Transaction Costs for Electronic Economic Exchanges

Because there is no third-party intermediary, Bitcoin transactions are purported to be substantially less expensive for users than those using traditional payments systems such as Paypal and traditional credit cards, which charge merchants significant fees for their role as trusted third party intermediary to validate electronic transactions. In addition, Bitcoin sales are *nonreversible*, which removes the possibility for misuse of consumer charge-backs, which merchants find costly. Merchants would presumably pass at least some of these savings on to the customer. While there is considerable anecdotal evidence that this is true, there are no comprehensive data on the size of Bitcoin's transaction cost advantage.

Some of the transaction cost advantage could be offset by the slow speed at which Bitcoin transactions currently occur, which, depending on the size of the transaction, can take a minimum of 10 minutes or as long as an hour.[13]

In addition, Bitcoin's advantage in transaction cost could be offset by the substantial volatility of Bitcoin's price. A rising dollar price of Bitcoin is likely to deter potential buyers who would expect to see their purchasing power be greater in the future. A falling Bitcoin price is likely to deter potential sellers who would expect to see their potential sales receipts be greater in the future.

Increased Privacy

Those who seek a heightened degree of privacy may find more comfort using Bitcoins for their (legal) commercial and financial transactions. The risk of identity theft may also be less, and some may find the removal of government from a monetary system attractive. However, as discussed above, Bitcoin transactions do not have the anonymity afforded by cash transactions, as there is a permanent and complete historical record of Bitcoin amounts and encrypted identities for all transactions on the Bitcoin system that is potentially traceable.

No Erosion of Purchasing Power by Inflation

Inflation is defined as a broad increase in the prices of goods and services. This is equivalent to saying that there is a fall in the value of the circulating currency. That fall in value means that each unit of the currency is exchangeable for a reduced amount of goods and services. Inflation is commonly thought to be a monetary phenomenon in which the supply of the currency outpaces the demand for the currency causing its unit value (in terms of what it can buy) to fall.

Most often governments (or their central bank) regulate the supply of money and credit and most often some degree of mismanagement of this government function is at the root of a persistent high inflation problem. In the case of Bitcoin, however, there is no government or central bank regulating the supply of Bitcoins. The supply of Bitcoins is programmed to grow at a steady rate regulated by the degree of mining activity (a process likely linked to a growing demand for Bitcoin) and then is capped at a fixed amount.

Inflation could occur if the demand for Bitcoin decreases relative to the fixed supply. Inflation could also occur if the Bitcoin network develops fractional reserve banking (i.e., banks that hold only a fraction of their deposits in reserve and lend out the rest), which would also be a vehicle that effectively increases the supply of circulating Bitcoins. If these digital banks move to a situation where held reserves stabilize, this source of inflation would diminish.

What Factors Might Deter Widespread Bitcoin Use?

There are a number of factors that could discourage widespread use of Bitcoin.

Not Legal Tender

The dollar is legal tender and by law can be used to extinguish public or private debts. A creditor is required to accept legal tender for the settlement of a debt. At a minimum, the payment of taxes forces U.S. individuals to hold dollars. Arguably, for many, such a government endorsement is comforting and creates a strong underlying demand for the dollar. By contrast, a currency like Bitcoin that is linked to a complex computer program that many do not understand and that operates without accountability to any controlling entity, could be an unattractive vehicle for holding wealth for many people.

Does Not Enjoy the Dollar's Network Externalities

As noted above, the attractiveness of using a dollar is dependent on the number of people already using it. Thus widespread use of the dollar encourages its continued use and is an impediment (although not an insurmountable barrier) to the use of other currencies, including Bitcoins.

Price Volatility Discourages Its Use as Medium of Exchange

Bitcoin's price has been volatile since its creation in 2009, subject to sharp appreciations and precipitous depreciations in value. However, 2013 has seen a much higher level of price fluctuation. During March and April of 2013, Bitcoin's dollar exchange rate moved from about $50 up to $350, and back to near $70. Bitcoin's price has moved up even more sharply during the fall of 2013, rising from near $50 in September to above $1,100 by early December and down to about $400 by April 2014. Since then Bitcoin's price had rebounded to about $600 by mid-July. This is a price pattern more typical of a commodity than of a currency to be used as a medium of exchange, and suggests the market for Bitcoin is currently being driven by speculative investors, not by a growing demand for Bitcoin due to increased transactions by traditional merchants and consumers.

The problem with having the Bitcoin network dominated by speculators is that it gives users an incentive to hoard Bitcoins rather than spend them—just the opposite of what would need to happen to make a currency a successful medium of exchange such as the dollar. [14]

Speculation could be more likely to dominate the market for Bitcoins because its value cannot be anchored to some underlying 'fundamental' such as an amount of some physical commodity such as gold, the value of an earnings stream that undergirds the price of a company's stock, or the perceived basic soundness and stability of an economy and its governing institutions (as is, arguably, true for the dollar).

The System's Long-Term Deflationary Bias Will Discourage Its Use as Currency

Because the supply is capped in the long run, widespread use of Bitcoin would mean that the demand for Bitcoin would likely outstrip supply, causing Bitcoin's price to steadily increase. The corollary of that increase is that the Bitcoin price of goods and services would steadily fall causing deflation. Faced with deflation, there is a strong incentive to hoard Bitcoins and not spend them, causing the current level of transactions to fall. [15]

If generalized to an economy-wide phenomenon deflation could cause slower than normal economic growth and higher than normal unemployment.

This possible outcome highlights the likely importance of the economy's principal currency being *elastic,* its supply increasing and decreasing to meet the changing needs of the economy, and of the important role of the central bank in implementing such a monetary policy. The perils of an inelastic currency were evident, for a period from about 1880 to 1914, when the United States monetary system operated under a gold standard. At this time, the deflationary bias of an inelastic supply of gold led to elevated real interest rates, caused periodic banking panics, and produced increased instability of output. The Federal Reserve was created in 1913 to provide an elastic currency. In particular, the generally good economic performance of the post-war era speaks to the benefits of having a central bank to administer an elastic currency, not only to meet the changing transaction needs of the economy, but also to proactively use monetary policy to stabilize output and inflation.

Bitcoins Networks Security Is Uncertain

While counterfeiting is purportedly not possible, Bitcoin exchanges and wallet services have at times struggled with security. Cash and traditional electronic payment systems also have periodic security problems, but a high incidence of security problems on a system trying to establish itself and gain customer confidence could be more damaging. Some notable examples of security breaches on the Bitcoin network have included the following:

- Hackers mounted a massive series of distributed denial-of-service (DDoS) attacks against the most popular Bitcoin exchange, Mt.Gox, in 2013. Mt. Gox subsequently declared bankruptcy.[16]
- In late August 2012, an operation titled Bitcoin Savings and Trust was shut down by the owner, allegedly leaving around 5.6 million USD in bitcoin-based debts.[17]
- In September 2012, Bitfloor, a Bitcoin exchange, reported being hacked, with 24,000 Bitcoins (roughly equivalent to 250,000 USD) stolen. As a result, Bitfloor temporarily suspended operations.[18]
- On April 3, 2013, Instawallet, a web-based wallet provider, was hacked, resulting in the theft of over 35,000 Bitcoins. With a price of 129.90 USD per b\Bitcoin at the time, or nearly 4.6 million USD in total, Instawallet suspended operations.[19]
- On August 11 2013, the Bitcoin Foundation announced that a bug in software within the Android operating system had been exploited to steal from users' wallets. [20]
- October 23 and 26, 2013, a Bitcoin bank, operated from Australia but stored on servers in the USA, was hacked, with a loss of 4,100 Bitcoins, or over 1 million AUD. [21]

Legal and Regulatory Issues

Legal Considerations Generally

In order to provide some information on recent efforts by federal, state, and international authorities to study, monitor, or regulate digital currencies, this section of the report (1) identifies the clause in the U.S. Constitution giving power to Congress over money; (2) describes some of the recent federal, state, and international activities and studies dealing with digital money; and (3) identifies some of the federal laws that might be implicated or that have been used with respect to digital money.

In providing this information, we have identified some federal statutes and regulatory regimes that may have some applicability to digital currency, although none contains explicit language to that effect or explicitly mentions currency not issued by a government authority. Some federal statutes, because of their broad coverage, are likely to be held by courts to apply in connection with digital currency. For example, courts are likely to hold that the federal criminal mail and wire fraud statutes apply to fraudulent schemes designed to result in monetary losses in connection with buying, selling, or trading digital currencies.[22] Federal statutes providing consumer protection with respect to consumer financial transactions, however, such as the Truth in Lending Act[23] and the Truth in Savings Act,[24] include no language specifically referencing digital currency transactions.[25]

Power of Congress under Article I of the U.S. Constitution

One of the direct powers of Congress under the U.S. Constitution, the grant of authority "to coin Money" and "regulate the Value thereof,"[26] appears to provide sufficient authority for extensive oversight and control of digital money. The Supreme Court has interpreted this clause broadly. It has been upheld to authorize legislation chartering the First Bank of the United States and giving it power to issue circulating notes.[27] Legislation requiring U.S. Treasury notes to be treated as legal tender for antecedent debts[28] and legislation that abrogated gold clauses in private contracts[29] have also been upheld on the basis of this clause of the Constitution. The breadth of the power can be discerned from a statement of the Court in the Legal Tender Cases when the Court opined that "[e]very contract for the payment of money simply is necessarily subject to the constitutional power of the government over the currency, whatever that power may be, and the obligation of the parties is therefore assumed with reference to that power."[30]

Recent Activity

This section provides a brief survey of some of the concerns and activities of federal, state, and international governmental entities with respect to the emergence of digital currencies.

Recent Legislative Activity: Congress

In Congress, interest in virtual currencies is at the exploratory stage. The Senate Finance Committee directed the Government Accountability Office

(GAO) to review any tax requirements and compliance risks implicated and to assess the Internal Revenue Service (IRS) efforts at informing the public in view of the offshore and internet sources of these currencies. On May 13, 2013, GAO released a survey[31] describing the types of virtual currencies, the inadequacy of available data on them, and the extent of IRS efforts. It noted that IRS guidance on virtual currencies[32] concentrates on currencies used in virtual communities, such as Linden Dollars in Second Life, and overlooks currencies, such as Bitcoin, that can be used in the real economy. GAO also notes that the tax code lacks clarity about how virtual currency is to be treated for reporting purposes. Is it property, barter, foreign currency, or a financial instrument?

The Senate Homeland Security and Governmental affairs Committee has begun to look into how federal agencies are confronting the rise of virtual currencies. On August 12, 2013, the Committee's Chairman and ranking Member sent letters[33] to several federal agencies, including the Departments of Justice (DOJ), the Treasury, and Homeland Security; the Securities and Exchange Commission (SEC); the Commodity Futures Trading Commission (CFTC); and the Federal Reserve, seeking information on their virtual currency policies, initiatives, activities, guidelines, or plans regarding virtual or digital currency. The committee envisions a government-wide approach to the threats and promises of digital currency.

Federal Reserve and European Central Bank Studies

At least one Federal Reserve economist is studying digital currencies and Bitcoin, in particular.[34] On the international front, the European Central Bank released a study[35] of virtual currencies that assesses both the prospects for growth and some of the potential problems that might accompany widespread use.

Federal Regulatory Activity

Federal regulatory activity includes guidance[36] issued by Treasury's Financial Crimes Enforcement Network (FINCEN) and a Winkelvoss Bitcoin Trust registration statement[37] filed with the Securities and Exchange (SEC) Commission. In addition, the SEC published an advisory[38] for investors on the threat of virtual currency scams on the Internet, filed a criminal fraud complaint[39] charging a Bitcoin exchange with engaging in a ponzi scheme, and successfully convinced a federal district court that Bitcoins are money. The court reasoned that because Bitcoins are used as money to purchase goods or services and can be exchanged for conventional currencies, they are money, and, thus, a contract for the investment of Bitcoins is an "investment contract," and, therefore, a security under federal securities law.[40] In another enforcement action, the Department of Homeland Security charged Mt. Gox, which is the Japanese-based largest Bitcoin exchange in the United States, with operating an unlicensed money services business in violation of 18 U.S.C. §1960 and seized its bank account.

State Regulatory Activity

State authorities moving in the direction of regulating virtual currencies are sometimes discovering problems in applying existing laws to the technological currencies. New York's Superintendent of Financial Services is investigating whether new regulation is needed and has issued subpoenas seeking information on a raft of virtual currencies.[41] California's Department of Business Oversight may have misdirected a cease and desist order to the Bitcoin Foundation because the Foundation confines itself to advocacy work.

APPLICABILITY OF SELECTED LAWS TO DIGITAL CURRENCY

Counterfeiting Criminal Statutes

The basic governmental interest in enacting laws against counterfeiting obligations of the United States is protecting the value of the dollar and the monetary system. Under title 18 U.S.C. §§470- 477 and 485-489 counterfeiting and forging of U.S. coins, currency, and obligations is subject to criminal sanctions, and under 18 U.S.C. §§478-483, criminal sanctions are prescribed for counterfeiting foreign coins, currency, and obligations. None of these statutes, however, applies expressly to a currency that exists only on the Internet and in computers in a digital form. Although the usual prosecution under these statutes involves attempts to replicate Federal Reserve notes or coins produced by the U.S. Mint, at least one case involved a conviction for issuing and circulating Liberty Dollars, designed as similar to but distinguishable from U.S. dollars and intended to "limit reliance on, and to compete with, United States currency."[42] Whether a digital currency, even if it is designed to attack the value of U.S. legal tender, could be prosecuted under the current language of these statutes is not clear.[43]

The Stamp Payments Act of 1862, 18 U.S.C. §336

The Stamp Payments Act makes it a crime to issue, circulate, or pay out "any note, check, memorandum, token or other obligation, for a less sum than $1, intended to circulate as money or to be received or used in lieu of lawful money of the United States." This law was enacted in 1862 to protect postage stamps from competition by private tokens. Congress had approved stamps as currency for fractions of $1 because metal coins were being hoarded and were virtually out of circulation.[44] It does not seem likely that a currency[45] that has no physicality would be held to be covered by this statute even though it circulates on the internet on a worldwide basis and is used for some payments of less than $1. The language of the statute, "not, check, memorandum, token," seems to contemplate a concrete object rather than a computer file; moreover, a digital currency such as Bitcoin, without a third-party issuer, cannot be said to be an obligation. However, there are some arguments that could be made, particularly should a digital currency become pervasive enough to be considered a possible competitor to U.S. official currency.[46]

The Electronic Fund Transfer Act, 15 U.S.C. §§1693 et seq.

The Electronic Fund Transfer Act (EFTA) establishes a framework for transfers of money electronically, but its coverage is limited in such a way that it appears not to be applicable to a digital currency in transactions involving no depository institution. EFTA specifically applies to transfers of funds initiated by electronic means from a consumer's account held at a financial institution. It covers transfers "initiated through an electronic terminal, telephonic instrument, or computer."[47] Its application is limited to deposit accounts "established primarily for personal, family, or household purposes,"[48] "held by a financial institution,"[49] with "financial institution" limited to banks, thrifts, savings associations, and credit unions.[50]

Federal Tax Law

Digital currencies have characteristics of traditional tax haven jurisdictions: earnings are not reported to the Internal Revenue Service (IRS) and users are provided some level of anonymity. Unlike traditional tax havens, however, digital currencies are able to operate without involving a financial institution.[51] The IRS provides limited guidance on the tax consequences of activities involving the virtual world. It cautions: "[i]n general, you can receive income in the form of money, property, or services. If you receive more income from the virtual world than you spend, you may be required to report the gain as taxable income. IRS guidance also applies when you spend more in a virtual world than you receive, you generally cannot claim a loss on an income tax return."[52] The guidance is limited and does not appear to target a digital currency such as Bitcoin that is used as a medium of exchange for goods and services in the real world. A Government Accountability Office (GAO) report earlier this year found inadequate IRS efforts to address tax implications of virtual currencies not used within a virtual economy.[53] As a step to counter misinformation circulating and the possibility for growth in such currencies, rather than recommending a costly rigorous compliance approach, GAO recommended that IRS "find relatively low-cost ways to provide information to taxpayers, such as the web statement IRS developed on virtual economies, on the basic tax reporting requirements for transactions using virtual currencies developed and used outside virtual economies."[54]

Federal Anti-Money Laundering Laws

Under the criminal anti-money laundering laws,[55] engaging in financial transactions that involve proceeds of illegal or terrorist activities or that are designed to finance such activities is prohibited. Money laundering crimes generally involve transactions processed by financial institutions, which is why the Bank Secrecy Act (BSA) imposes various recordkeeping requirements on banks and other financial institutions.[56] Under the Currency and Foreign Transaction Reporting Act[57] component of the BSA, financial institutions must file reports of cash transactions exceeding amounts set by the Secretary of the Treasury in regulations, and file suspicious activity reports (SARs) for transactions meeting a certain monetary threshold or intended to evade reporting requirements. Financial institutions, as required by the Secretary of the Treasury, must also develop and follow anti-money laundering programs and customer identification programs. All of these requirements apply to "money services businesses" (MSBs), a category of financial institution which must register with the Department of the Treasury.[58] MSBs include a variety of businesses, including dealers in foreign exchange, check cashers, traveler's check issuers, providers of prepaid access cards, and money transmitters.[59] These entities must register with the

Department of the Treasury and comply with BSA requirements. On March 18, 2013, FINCEN issued interpretative guidance[60] requiring Bitcoin exchanges— individuals and businesses that change Bitcoins into U.S. or foreign currency into Bitcoins—to register as money services businesses pursuant to the BSA.

Federal Securities Regulation

Securities regulation may focus on two different legal issues involving Bitcoins—investments purchased with Bitcoins and investing in Bitcoins.

Investments Purchased with Bitcoins

The United States District Court for the Eastern District of Texas held in August 2013 that it had subject matter jurisdiction over possible fraud in investments purchased with Bitcoins because of its determination that investments purchased with Bitcoins are securities.[61] The Securities and Exchange Commission (SEC) alleged that the defendant had violated provisions of the Securities Act of 1933[62] and the Securities Exchange Act of 1934[63] and had conducted a kind of Ponzi scheme. According to the facts stated by the SEC, the defendant, Trendon T. Shavers, who was the founder and operator of Bitcoin Savings and Trust (BTCST), had "made a number of solicitations aimed at enticing lenders to invest in Bitcoin-related investment opportunities." Shavers had advertised that he sold Bitcoins and that he would pay an investor up to 1% interest daily until the investor withdrew the funds or until BTCST could no longer be profitable. Investors lost a considerable amount of money, and the SEC brought suit. Shavers defended that the BTCST investments were not securities under federal securities laws because Bitcoins are not money and are not regulated by the United States. Shavers seemed also to argue that, because the investments were not securities, the court had no jurisdiction over a lawsuit alleging violations of the federal securities laws. The SEC argued that the BTCST investments were investment contracts, thus bringing them within the definition of "securities" and therefore subject to regulation by the SEC.

The court held that it did have jurisdiction over the case because of its determination that investments purchased with Bitcoins are securities. 15 U.S.C. section 77b defines a "security" in a very broad way as "any note, stock, treasury stock, security future, security-based swap, bond ... [or] investment contract." Cases such as SEC v. W.J. Howey & Co[64] and Long v.

Schultz Cattle Co.[65] have set out a kind of template for an investment contract: An investment contract involves (1) an investment of money (2) in a common enterprise (3) with the expectation of profits from the efforts of a promoter or a third party. Thus, according to the court, it had to determine whether the BTCST investments were an investment of money. The court found that, because Bitcoins can be used to purchase goods or services and even used to pay for individual living expenses, they are a "currency or form of money" and that "investors wishing to invest in BTCST provided an investment of money." The court also found that there was a common enterprise because the investors were dependent upon Shavers's expertise in Bitcoin markets and that Shavers promised a significant return on their investments. Finally, the Eastern District of Texas found that the third prong of the investment contract template was met because the BTCST investors had an expectation of deriving profits from their investments. Because it found that the BTCST investments satisfied the investment contract definition, the court held that it had subject matter jurisdiction over possible fraud in investments purchased with Bitcoins.

Investing in Bitcoins

Investing in bitcoins may trigger regulation by the SEC. For example, it has been reported that Cameron and Tyler Winkelvoss are forming a public exchange-traded fund (ETF) for bitcoins and have filed paperwork with the SEC.[66] The ETF may be traded on a major exchange and open to retail investors. According to the SEC's website, an ETF is often registered as an open-end investment company or unit investment trust under the Investment Company Act of 1940. The regulatory requirements for ETFs include the following:

> As investment companies, ETFs are subject to the regulatory requirements of the federal securities laws as well as certain exemptions that are necessary for ETFs to operate under those laws. Together, the federal securities laws and the relevant exemptions apply requirements that are designed to protect investors from various risks and conflicts associated with investing in ETFs.
>
> For example, ETFs, like mutual funds, are subject to statutory limitations on their use of leverage and transactions with affiliates. ETFs also are subject to specific reporting requirements and disclosure obligations relating to investment objectives, risks, expenses, and other information in their registration statements and periodic reports.
>
> In addition, ETFs are subject to oversight by boards of directors.[67]

Commodity Futures Trading Commission Regulation

The Commodity Futures Trading Commission (CFTC) has authority to regulate commodities futures and their markets and certain foreign exchange instruments. It is possible that CFTC could conclude that a digital currency such as Bitcoins falls within the Commodity Exchange Act's (CEA's) definition of "commodity," which includes a catch-all phrase—"and all other goods and articles."[68] There is also the possibility that the CFTC could include such a digital currency within its foreign exchange regulations because the CEA does not define "foreign currency" or "foreign exchange," although it covers and defines "foreign-exchange forwards" and "foreign-exchange swaps."[69]

INTERNATIONAL LEGAL ISSUES

Because digital currency knows no national boundaries, it may require an international solution and, thus, has drawn the attention of international regulators. Traditional payment systems which involve monetary systems are set up in statutes and regulations and overseen by central banks and transactions processed by banks and other authorized or chartered financial institutions. With virtual currencies, however, no laws and regulations define the duties and obligations of parties, provide for finality of settlement, resolution of disputes, or supervision of services provided. One recent study of digital currencies by the European Central Bank is premised on the possibility that growth of digital currencies will carry with it a need for international cooperation in developing a regulatory framework.[70] According to the report, the current level of virtual currencies poses little risk to price stability; there are, however, risks to users and a potential for criminal schemes.[71] According to the report, neither the European Monetary Directive nor the European Payment Services Directive clearly applies to virtual currencies such as Bitcoin.[72]

Concern About International Monetary Fund Authority

One issue that has received some attention is the ability of the International Monetary Fund (IMF) to defend a traditional currency of one of its member countries from a speculative attack involving a digital currency such as Bitcoin since the IMF's Articles of Agreement do not explicitly permit it to acquire a currency not issued by one of its members. There is at least one commentary examining possible options for amending or reinterpreting the IMF's authority.

End Notes

[1] On November 18, the Senate committee on Homeland Security and Governmental Affairs held a hearing on: Beyond Silk Road: Potential Risks, Threats, and Promises, available at http://www.hsgac.senate.gov/hearings/beyond-silkroad-potential-risks-threats-and-promises-of-virtual-currencies. On November 19, the Senate Committee on Banking, Housing, and Urban Affairs held a hearing on: The Current and Future Impact of Virtual Currencies, available at http://www.banking.senate.gov/public/index.cfm?FuseAction =Hearings.Hearing&Hearing_ID=955322cc-d648-4a00- a41f-c23be8ff4cad.

[2] General background discussions about Bitcoin can be found at Bitcoin, available at http://bitcoin.org/en/; Jerry Brito and Andrea Castillo, Bitcoin: a Primer for Policymakers, Mercatus Center, George Mason University, 2013, available at http://mercatus. org/publication/bitcoin-primer-policymakers; and Federal Reserve Bank of Chicago, Chicago Fed Letter, Bitcoin: A Primer, 2013, available at http://www.chicagofed. org/ digital_assets/publications/chicago_fed_letter/ 2013/cfldecember2013_317.pdf.

[3] The current price of a Bitcoin can be obtained from Bitcoin-Charts available at http://bitcoincharts.com/.

[4] Joshua Brustein, "Bitcoin May Not Be Anonymous After All," Bloomberg Business Week, August 27, 2013, available at http://www.businessweek.com/articles/2013-08-27/bitcoin-may-not-be-so-anonymous-after-all.

[5] Sarah Meiklejohn, Marjori Pomarole, Grant Jordan, Kirill Levchenko, Damon McCoy, Geoffrey M. Voelker, and Stefan Savage, "A Fist Full of Bitcoins: Characterizing Payments Among Men with No Name," University of California, San Diego, December 2013, available at http://cseweb.ucsd.edu/~smeiklejohn/.

[6] Bitcoin data from Bitcoin Charts, available at http://bitcoincharts.com/.

[7] Board of Governors of the Federal Reserve System, Money Stock Measures(H.6), available at http://www.federalreserve.gov/releases/h6/current/default.htm.

[8] Visa, Inc., Fact Sheet, available at http://corporate.visa.com/_media/visa-fact-sheet.pdf.

[9] Bank for International Settlements, "Foreign Exchange Turnover in April 2013: Preliminary Global Results," Triennial Central Bank Survey, September 2013, https://www. bis.org/publ/rpfx13fx.pdf.

[10] See also: European Central Bank, Virtual Currency Schemes, October 2012, pp33-39, available at http://www.ecb.europa.eu/pub/pdf/other/virtualcurrencyschemes201210en.pdf.

[11] In a recent letter to the Senate Committee on Homeland Security and Governmental Affairs, Fed Chairman Bernanke noted that virtual currencies have the potential to be beneficial, but also carry risks, and while not a direct regulatory responsibility, are monitored by the Fed. He did not express any concern about virtual currencies hindering the Fed's ability to conduct monetary policy. Available at http://online.wsj.com/public/resources/documents/ VCurrenty111813.pdf.

[12] Varian, Hal R., 2003, "Economics of Information Technology," in "Academic Papers and Books, 2004 and Earlier Non-technical papers," available at http://www.sims. berkeley. edu/~hal.

[13] See Data on transaction times at Blockchain, available at http://blockchain.info/charts/avg-confirmation-time.

[14] Felix Salmon, "The Bitcoin Bubble and the Future of Currency," Medium, April 2013, available at https://medium.com/money-banking/2b5ef79482cb.

[15] Dan Kervick, "Bitcoin's Deflationary Weirdness," New Economic Perspectives, April 2013, available at http://neweconomicperspectives.org/2013/04/talking-bitcoin.html.

[16] Mitt Clinch, "Bitcoin Hacked: Price Stumbles After Buying Frenzy," CNBC, April 4, 2013, available at http://www.cnbc.com/id/100615508.

[17] Adrianne Jeffries, "Suspected Multi-Million Dollar Bitcoin Pyramid Scheme Shuts Down, Investors Revolt," The Verge, August 27, 2012, available at http://www.theverge.com/2012/8/27/3271637/bitcoin-savings-trust-pyramidscheme-shuts-down.

[18] Vitalik Burterin, "Bitfloor Hacked, $250,000 Missing," Bitcoin Magazine, Sept 4, 2012, available at http://bitcoinmagazine.com/2139/bitfloor-hacked-250000-missing/.

[19] Joe Weisenthal, "Bitcoin Service Instawallet: We've Been Hacked and are Suspending Service Indefinitely," Business Insider, April 3, 2013, available at http://www.businessinsider.com/instawallet-suspended-2013-4.

[20] Richard Chirgwen, "Android Bug Batters Bitcoin Wallets," The Register, August 12, 2013, available at http://www.theregister.co.uk/2013/08/12/android_bug_batters_bitcoin_wallets/.

[21] Ben Grubb, "Australian Bitcoin Bank Hacked: $1 Million + Stolen," Brisbane Times, November 8, 2013, available at http://www.brisbanetimes.com.au/it-pro/security-it/australian-bitcoin-bank-hacked-1m-stolen-20131108-hv2iv.html.

[22] These include 18 U.S.C. §§1341 (mail fraud) and 1343 (wire fraud). The wire fraud statute, for example, applies to "[w]hoever, having devised or intending to devise any scheme or artifice to defraud, or for obtaining money or property by means of false or fraudulent pretenses, representations, or promises, transmits or causes to be transmitted by means of wire, radio, or television communication in interstate or foreign commerce, any writings, signs, signals, pictures, or sounds for the purpose of executing such scheme or artifice." Regulation Z, 12 C.F.R. 226, implementing the Truth in Lending Act (TILA) is premised on credit transactions, interest, and fees in terms of U.S. money. At present it is a matter of pure speculation as to whether the Consumer Financial Protection Board (CFPB), the agency charged with implementing TILA, could reasonably interpret the statute, given its language, structure, and legislative history, as a basis for issuing regulations to cover transactions in digital money.

[23] 15 U.S.C. §§1601 et seq.

[24] 12 U.S.C. §§4301-4313. (This applies to deposits held at depository institutions, i.e., banks, thrifts, savings associations, and credit unions.).

[25] A list of the regulations implementing federal laws providing consumer protection for financial transactions can be found on the Consumer Financial Protection Bureau's website at http://www.consumerfinance.gov/regulations/#ecfr,\.

[26] U.S. Const., art. I, §8, cl. 5.

[27] McCulloch v. Maryland, 17 U.S. (4 Wheat.) 316 (1819); Veazie Bank v. Fenno, 75 U.S. (8 Wall.) 533 (1869).

[28] Legal Tender Cases (Knox v. Lee), 79 U.S. (12 Wall.) 457(1871); Juilliard v. Greenman, 110 U.S. 421 (1884).

[29] Norman v. Baltimore & Ohio R.R., 294 U.S. 240 (1935).

[30] Legal Tender Cases (Knox v. Lee), 79 U.S. (12 Wall.) 457, 549 (1871).

[31] U.S. Government Accountability Office, "Virtual Economies and Currencies: Additional IRS Guidance Could Reduce Tax Compliance Risks" (May 2013).

[32] Internal Revenue Service, "Tax Consequences of Virtual World Transactions," http://www.irs.gov/Businesses/SmallBusinesses-&-Self-Employed/Tax-Consequences-of-Virtual-World-Transactions.

[33] http://www.hsgac.senate.gov/reports/letters

[34] François R. Velde, "Bitcoin: A primer," Chicago Fed Letter (December 2013). http://www.chicagofed.org/ digital_assets/publications/chicago_fed_letter/2013/cfldecember2013_317.pdf.

[35] European Central Bank, "Virtual Currency Schemes," (October 2012). http://www.google.com/url?sa=t&rct=j&q=& esrc=s&frm=1&source=web&cd=1&ved=0CCsQFjAA&url=http%3A%2F%2Fwww.ecb.europa.eu%2Fpub%2Fpdf%2Fother%2Fvirtualcurrencyschemes201210en.pdf&ei=UiCUp_HGoqqsQSJ0YCICQ&usg=AFQjCNHPyKEw4gnOcQ27d-znAvyPmONT3g&bvm=bv.56146854,d.cWc.

[36] U.S. Department of the Treasury, Financial Crimes Enforcement Network, "Application of FinCEN's Regulations to Persons Administering, Exchanging, or Using Virtual Currencies," (March 18, 2013), http://www.fincen.gov/ statutes_regs/guidance/html/FIN-2013-G001.html.

[37] Form S-1 Registration Statement, Winkelvoss Bitcoin Trust. http://www. sec.gov/Archives/ edgar/data/1579346/ 000119312513279830/d562329ds1.htm.

[38] U.S. Securities and Exchange Commission Press Release 2013-132, "SEC Charges Texas Man with Running Bitcoin-Denominated Ponzi Scheme," (July 23, 2013). http://www.sec.gov/News/PressRelease/Detail/PressRelease/ 1370539730583.

[39] http://www.sec.gov/litigation/complaints/2013/comp-pr2013-132.pdf.

[40] Securities and Exchange Commission v. Shavers, 2013 WL4028182, No. 4:13-CV-416 (E.D. Tex. Aug. 6, 2013). This appears to be the first ruling addressing the question of whether digital currency issued without the backing of a government or other official entity is to be legally considered money.

[41] New York State, Department of Financial Services, "Notice of Inquiry on Virtual Currencies," August 12, 2013. http://www.dfs.ny.gov/about/press2013/memo1308121.pdf.

[42] Derek A. Dion, "Defendant Convicted of Minting His Own Currency," Press Release, U.S. Attorney's Office, Western District of North Carolina (March 18, 2011). http://www.fbi.gov/charlotte/press-releases/2011/defendantconvicted-of-minting-his-own-currency.

[43] For a discussion, see, "I'll Gladly Trade You Two Bits on Tuesday for a Byte Today: Bitcoin, Regulating Fraud in the E-conomy of Hacker Cash," 2013 University of Illinois Journal of Law, Technology and Policy (Spring 2013).

[44] For further exposition of the genesis, legislative history, and analysis of the Stamp Payments Act, including the possibility that it may apply to electronic currency, see Thomas P. Vartanian, Robert H. Ledig, and Yolanda Demianczuk, "Echoes of the Past with Implications for the Future: The Stamp Payments Act of 1862 and Electronic Commerce", 67 BNA's Banking Report (September 23, 1996).

[45] Virtual currencies, such as Linden Dollars, are not likely to conflict with this statute because they do not appear to "circulate as money or be received in lieu of lawful money," within the meaning of the statute. They circulate only in a limited environment and are redeemable only in virtual goods, and, thus, are similar to the tokens and tickets redeemable in goods and services on a limited basis that courts have found not to have been issued in violation of

the Stamp Payments Act. United States v. Monongahela Bridge Co., 26 F. Cas. 1292 (W.D. Pa. 1863) (No. 15796); United States v. Roussopulous, 95 F. 977 (D. Minn. 1899).

[46] See Vartanian, et al., supra, n. 8, and Reuben Grinberg, "Bitcoin: An Innovative Digital Currency, 5 Hastings Science & Technology Law Journal 159 (2012).

[47] 15 U.S.C. §1693a(6).

[48] 15 U.S.C. §1693a(2).

[49] 15 U.S.C. §1693a(2).

[50] 15 U.S.C. §1693a(11).

[51] For further information see, Marian, Omri, "Are Cryptocurrencies Super Tax Havens?," 112 Michigan Law Review First Impressions 38 (2013).

[52] Internal Revenue Service, "Tax Consequences of Virtual World Transactions," http://www.irs.gov/Businesses/SmallBusinesses-&-Self-Employed/Tax-Consequences-of-Virtual-World-Transactions.

[53] U.S. Government Accountability Office, "Virtual Economies and Currencies: Additional IRS Guidance Could Reduce Tax Compliance Risk," (May 2013).

[54] U.S. Government Accountability Office, "Virtual Economies and Currencies: Additional IRS Guidance Could Reduce Tax Compliance Risk," 17 (May 2013).

[55] 18 U.S.C. §§1956 and 1957.

[56] Titles I and II of P.L. 91-508, including 12 U.S.C. §§1829b, and 1951-1959; 31 U.S.C. §§5311 et seq.

[57] 31 U.S.C. §§5311 et seq.

[58] Bank Secrecy Act requirements for money services businesses are listed on the Financial Crimes Enforcement Network's website at http://www.fincen.gov/financial_ institutions/msb/msbrequirements.html.

[59] 31 C.F.R. §1010.100(ff).

[60] U.S. Department of the Treasury, Financial Crimes Enforcement Network, "Application of FinCEN's Regulations to Persons Administering, Exchanging, or Using Virtual Currencies," (March 18, 2013), http://www.fincen.gov/ statutes_regs/guidance/html/FIN-2013-G001.html.

[61] Securities and Exchange Commission v. Shavers, No. 4:13-CV-416 (E.D. Tex. Aug. 6, 2013).

[62] 15 U.S.C. §§77a et seq.

[63] 15 U.S.C. §§78a et seq.

[64] 328 U.S. 293 (1946).

[65] 881 F.2d 129 (5th Cir. 1989).

[66] http://qz/99632/winkelvoss-bitcoin-etf-risk-factors.

[67] sec.gov/investor/alerts/etfs.pdf.

[68] 7 U.S.C. §1a(9). It reads: The term "commodity" means wheat, cotton, rice, corn, oats, barley, rye, flaxseed, grain sorghums, mill feeds, butter, eggs, Solanum tuberosum (Irish potatoes), wool, wool tops, fats and oils (including lard, tallow, cottonseed oil, peanut oil, soybean oil, and all other fats and oils), cottonseed meal, cottonseed, peanuts, soybeans, soybean meal, livestock, livestock products, and frozen concentrated orange juice, and all other goods and articles, except onions (as provided by section 13–1 of this title) and motion picture box office receipts (or any index, measure, value, or data related to such receipts), and all services, rights, and interests (except motion picture box office receipts, or any index, measure, value or data related to such receipts) in which contracts for future delivery are presently or in the future dealt in.

[69] 7 U.S.C. §§1a(24) and (25).

[70] European Central Bank, "Virtual Currency Schemes," (October 2012). http://www.ecb.europa.eu/pub/pdf/other/ virtualcurrencyschemes201210en.pdf. (Hereinafter, European Central Bank Report.)

[71] European Central Bank, "Virtual Currency Schemes," (October 2012). http://www.ecb.europa.eu/pub/pdf/other/ virtualcurrencyschemes201210en.pdf. (Hereinafter, European Central Bank Report.)

[72] European Central Bank Report, at 43. The report notes noted that there are attempts in some of the countries belonging to the European Union to develop a means of regulating such currencies. Apparently courts in France are looking into whether Bitcoin transactions are subject to electronic money regulations. See Finextra.http://www.finextra. com/news/ fullstory.aspx?newsitemid=22921.

INDEX

C

D

E

F

G

H

I

J

L

M

N

O

P

Q

R

S

T

U

V

W